Praise for *Unstoppable*

"Many people don't change because they feel deep down that change isn't possible. So if we want greater happiness and success in our lives, we need to kick-start the belief that we can change. In *Unstoppable*, Tracy Timm outlines clear and practical ways to break out of the cycle of feeling stuck so you can get more wins, which will help you to pursue your long-term goals and dreams."

SHAWN ACHOR, *New York Times*–bestselling author of *The Happiness Advantage* and *Big Potential*

"Changing careers is daunting. Tracy Timm's *Unstoppable* provides the framework you never knew you needed to take the guess-work out of the transition."

LAURA GASSNER OTTING, author of *Limitless*

"Start now, start today. *Unstoppable* provides a simple, proven, effective method to find career clarity and build a life that matters."

ADAM SMILEY POSWOLSKY, author of *The Quarter-Life Breakthrough*

"*Unstoppable* is the career guidebook for anyone wishing there was a method to the work madness. In her proven formula, Tracy Timm teaches you about effective introspection—how to find the Venn diagram overlap of all the traits and skills you bring to the table—and how to create an action plan to successfully transition careers. If you've been looking for the missing manual on how to drive your career forward, this is it."

LISA LEWIS MILLER, CEO of GetCareerClarity.com

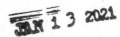

"So often books talk about what your passion or purpose is, or why it's so important to pursue it—but never tell you how to find it and how to do it for yourself. With this practical, tools-driven book, Tracy Timm gives you all three. A vision to pursue, a reason to pursue it, and, most importantly, step-by-step guidance on how to find—and do—what makes you unstoppable."

TAMSEN WEBSTER, founder and chief message strategist of Find the Red Thread

"If you want to chase your one singular passion to end all passions, then this isn't the book for you. However, if you want to lead a much more fulfilling, purposeful life filled with excitement (and passion) for your work, then *Unstoppable* is exactly the book to get you started."

SCOTT ANTHONY BARLOW, CEO and founder of Happen to Your Career

"*Unstoppable* by Tracy Timm is a heartfelt, entertaining, and informative read, full of actionable tools and techniques that are sure to leave you energized and ready to tackle your future from the minute you dive in. I highly recommend this book for anyone who desires to unlock their true potential and live their best life."

JEFF HOFFMAN, cofounder of Priceline

"In today's complex world, where we invest our precious time matters more than ever. This book is a powerful blueprint to help you maximize your personal and professional time. If you're looking to make a bigger impact, be fulfilled, and truly live out your dreams, I highly recommend you read *Unstoppable*."

ERIN KING, social media expert and speaker

UNSTOPPABLE

DISCOVER YOUR **TRUE VALUE,**

DEFINE YOUR **GENIUS ZONE,** AND

DRIVE YOUR **DREAM CAREER**

TRACY TIMM

PAGE TWO
BOOKS

Cataloguing in publication information is available from Library and Archives Canada.
ISBN 978-1-989603-45-1 (paperback)
ISBN 978-1-989603-76-5 (ebook)

Page Two
www.pagetwo.com

Cover and interior design by Taysia Louie
Interior illustrations by Taysia Louie and Fiona Lee
Printed and bound in Canada by Friesens
Distributed in Canada by Raincoast Books
Distributed in the US and internationally
by Publishers Group West, a division of Ingram

20 21 22 23 24   5 4 3 2 1

unstoppablecareerbook.com

To everyone I've told over the last ten years

that I was working on a book . . . I wasn't lying, after all.

CONTENTS

"Don't ask yourself what the world needs. Ask yourself what makes you come alive, and go do that, because what the world needs is people who have come alive."

HOWARD THURMAN

INTRODUCTION
THE AWAKENING

THIS IS A book about discovering, defining, and driving your ideal career—finding the professional pursuit in which you can be and feel unstoppable. In the following pages, I've laid out my tested and proven method for this type of clarity called the Nth Degree. These steps will guide you in identifying and capitalizing on a career uniquely suited to you. As you follow the process laid out in this book, you will become hyper-focused on your niche in the marketplace— that sweet spot where you can love what you do, perform at the highest level of your craft, do something meaningful in the world, and, of course, get paid. This level of career clarity will allow you to experience wealth in more ways than one— through finances, freedom, *and* fulfillment.

If that sounds fantastical to you right now, I can relate. I used to feel the same way, and throughout this book, I share many examples from my journey that prove this to be true. But thankfully, one day, I had a serendipitous experience that proved to me that work didn't have to suck. That day, I witnessed someone come *alive* just *talking* about his ideal career. That's when I learned the difference between the careers that we settle for because we think we have to and the ideal professional experience that we could have. It was this first encounter with someone explaining his ideal career that allowed me to believe in its possibility and pursue mine with intention.

My Unexpected First Career

In the fall of 2010, I began my first job working for an investment bank headquartered just outside of the financial mecca of New York City. As a psychology major, I had never expected to land this position, but I had grown to believe it would prove my success or failure as a professional. After all, I had beat out several of my classmates who would have given a limb to work at a hallowed desk on Wall Street.

My role as an analyst began as many others have, with my fellow new hires competing for the highest scores in training and jockeying for the best desks on the trading floor. Despite my best efforts to master bond math and negotiate the social strata of the trading floor culture, I always felt like an outsider. Every morning, as I commuted the four minutes from my apartment to the towering glass bank building, I attempted to convince myself that today I would understand more of what was going on or I would feel less like an outcast. Time marched on, but no matter how hard I worked or how savvy I became, the ugly truth was staring me in the face. This reality became so loud and so unbearable that just two years into this position, I could no longer ignore it.

I was absolutely, unapologetically, direly, hopelessly *miserable* at work.

Luckily, this anguished existence proved to be the necessary context for me to finally understand what work *could* be, instead of what I believed it *had* to be. But I needed to see an up-close example of this alternate reality to create that belief.

Life on the Trading Floor

Working on a Wall Street trading floor is a unique experience. Sure, you can watch movies like *Wall Street* and *Boiler Room* to get a general sense of the environment, but there's really nothing that can prepare you for life "on the desk." I won't be making any *Wolf of Wall Street* references here, but let's just say that the setting is intense. Imagine a room the length of two football fields and about half as wide, with a ceiling at least fifty feet high. An aisle runs perfectly down the middle, and on each side are row upon row of desks that meet the walls. Individual sets of computer screens, phone turrets, and Bloomberg keyboards are positioned in the middle of the desks, butting up against the same setup on the other side of the desk where another employee sits. All you needed to do was stand up, and you'd be towering over the person in front of you just trying to get through the day.

By 2012, I was working as a salesperson on the credit desk. I sold (or more accurately "facilitated the trading of") high-yield and distressed bonds and other loan investments to institutional investors and hedge funds. In two years, I had learned many important lessons about life on the trading floor. You're allowed to make a mistake, but you're not allowed to make the same mistake twice. If someone wants to make a bet on how many push-ups the intern can do or whether or not they can eat one of everything in the vending machine, just go with it. And if you want to keep your job (and you don't want to be verbally harangued or have a beverage thrown at you), never, *ever* miss a trade.

At first, that last point didn't seem challenging, because it was my job, after all. However, trading could only be done at your desk, so this rule required your physical presence at your desk at all times. That meant that I was to remain seated in front of my four computer screens for approximately twelve hours per day. I ate breakfast and lunch there. My trips to the bathroom lasted five minutes or less. I didn't take an afternoon break for the entire first year. But as my misery grew, my leash lengthened. That's when my friend, Joe, and I started a coffee-break routine in the lull hours of the afternoon. At three p.m., like clockwork, we ascended the escalator to the outdoor terrace on the eighth floor, made one lap around it, and returned to our desks. The entire break took little more than five minutes, but some days, it was the only activity that got me through the slog. Poetically, it was during one of these breaks that I experienced a moment that proved to be both life and career changing.

The Five-Minute Break That Changed Everything

One day, while my closest coworker and I were walking on the terrace, scanning the usual scenery that surrounded the building, I noticed something different. On a bridge visible from the roof of the building, a handful of construction workers had gathered to do some repairs. I felt tired of our usual "I hate my job and I feel stuck" conversation, so I used this bridge to pivot. Without expecting much more than a grunt of acknowledgment, I said, "Hey, check that out. Looks like they're doing some kind of construction on the bridge . . ."

Those were the last words I spoke in that conversation. As soon as my terrace buddy, Joe, caught sight of the bridge, he immediately cut me off. Much to my surprise, words started spilling out of him. "Wow, okay! Well, there's so much to take into consideration. I mean, the bridge looks like it's made of concrete so it's probably a beam bridge, which means it's going to be fairly strong when it comes to compression but weak when it comes to tension. So, they will likely add steel bars to reinforce it, but depending on the time of year and what the concrete is made of, the bridge will expand or contract. The engineers have to adjust the composite structures of the bridge to make sure that the tension and strength is still in balance and..."

I stopped in my tracks.

As Joe kept talking, I observed him: his eyes were alert, alive, and brighter; his body language had shifted, his chest lifted and stance strengthened. Even his gestures became more expressive and intense than I had ever seen. I slowly realized that I was witnessing the stream of consciousness that comes from someone purely engaged in a subject that sparks passion and intrigue in them—someone experiencing the flow of being completely immersed in a topic and energized by that focus. He was straight-up *gushing*! About bridges!

Honestly, it scared the living hell out of me.

Here was this human being—someone I thought I knew—who I had worked with *every* day of *every* week of *every* month for an entire *year*, and I had never (seriously, never) seen him behave in this way. In all our time spent building models, looking at credits, talking about trades, and working twelve hours a day, I had never once seen Joe even one-hundredth as interested as he was in that random bridge. It was all I could do to not physically shake him back to normal.

I could hold in my shock no longer. "I'm sorry, what?! Bridges?!" I yelled. "You obviously love this stuff, and all we ever talk about is how much we hate our jobs and how stuck we feel here. What in the *hell* are you doing at a job like this when you so obviously love construction and engineering?"

Why the strong reaction? I'll be honest, once my momentary shock subsided, I was livid. The only reason I was still working at the bank (or at least the only reason I allowed

myself to believe) was that I had no idea what I was passionate about or what I really wanted to do. I would have happily
run out the front door if I had a pursuit that resonated as
deeply as his seemed to be. I wanted that. And he had it. So,
in my mind, someone had some 'splaining to do.

"Well," he said, "here's the deal. I studied engineering in
college. And I absolutely love construction. But you know
how it is. *This*," he said, gesturing to the building, "*this* is what
successful people do. I can't be in construction. I *have* to stay
here. It's what I *should* do. It's the *only way* I can make really
good money. And most of all, it's what people *expect* me to do."

Escaping the Shoulds That Keep Us Stuck

I still shudder thinking about that moment.

> Successful people
> Should
> The only way
> Expectation

I had been telling myself those exact excuses for two years.
I had been keeping my growing cognitive dissonance at bay
by convincing myself that I had no choice. If I wanted to be
successful in life, it *had* to be there. However, thanks to the
human mirror standing in front of me, I began to question the
validity of everything I believed about work:

> Are *successful people* really this miserable?
> *Should* I really dread going to work every day?
> Is Wall Street the *only way* to make "good money"?
> Is this really what people *expect* of me?

What sealed the deal on challenging these beliefs, you may wonder. No sooner had Joe graced me with this shining example of hope than his flow state began to drain away. My friend slowly but surely reverted back to what he was accustomed to: feeling jaded and disillusioned, sucking it up, and accepting his "fate." I could see the change in him physically and sense it in him mentally. In that moment, I decided *no*. That was not going to be me.

I had been given a gift. I had seen the other side. I had watched in real time as someone accessed the best professional version of himself and then let it fade as his limiting beliefs and the external expectations kept him from living that way full-time. No matter what happened next, I was not going to allow myself to waste away in a place that robbed me of my potential and made me feel dead inside.

The Journey to My Dream Job

What followed for me was anything but a linear path. It's not like I had this insight, ran out the front door, discovered my dream job, and lived happily ever after. That wouldn't exactly make for much of a book, and it sure as hell wouldn't be all that relatable. Instead, I spent the next two years, and more money than I care to admit, in pursuit of my ideal career. It was this journey, the lessons learned therein, and the application of that knowledge for like-minded professionals who were struggling that became the basis of my proven career clarity methodology, the Nth Degree. Through many humbling experiences, valuable mentors, mini failures, and macro lessons, I finally found my professional niche. When I looked back, I saw that I'd done everything a person needs to do to discover their ideal career—I'd just done it inefficiently and out of order. Once I sat down and clarified those necessary steps of introspection and exploration, and I tested them out with willing and eager students and clients, I realized that I'd discovered exactly what our generation needs: a step-by-step, proven, tried-and-true strategy for career clarity.

With this methodology, I've been able to accomplish a few amazing things:

1 I'm a proud owner of my own business.

2 I trademarked the Nth Degree—the only proven, end-to-end, career clarity program of its kind.

3 I became a career advisor to hundreds of professionals who have discovered their ideal careers.

4 I also served as a human capital advisor to hundreds of fast-growing companies.

5 I launched a successful career as a paid professional speaker.

6 And (spoiler alert) I wrote a book!

I never could have even imagined any of this without first becoming aware of the fact that I was settling—I'd gone all in on the job, role, industry, or career that I felt *expected* to pursue. The way I believed work *had* to be in order for my life or career to be considered successful. And the less-than-ideal pursuits that I learned to accept as inevitable and that ultimately kept me stuck.

Wake Up in Your Career Journey

I wrote this book to prove to you that you do not have to accept your current work situation as your fate. You're also not behind, lost, stuck, or a failure. Instead, if you're willing to challenge some of your limiting beliefs and let go of the expectations of others, you can start to pursue *your ideal career*—a profession that honors your values, embraces your gifts, and leverages your expertise. The path to get there—the step-by-step strategy to discover, define, and drive a career you love—is simple and replicable. This is the Nth Degree process. It might not be easy, but it is straightforward, tangible, and achievable, if you follow these seven steps to (a) discover your true value, (b) define your genius zone, and (c) drive your dream career.

The Seven Steps in the Nth Degree Methodology
Now
Nature
Nurture
Niche
Network
Navigate
Nourish

By using the tools I offer at each of these steps, you will destroy doubt and fear, clearly determine and articulate your vision, and become empowered with the confidence to turn your dreams into reality. It's that simple. Rather, it *can be* that simple, if you follow along with me.

In the following chapters, I invite you to apply the proven methodology used in the Nth Degree workshops, coaching programs, and online courses to transform your career from stuck to unstoppable. If you lean in and embrace each lesson, this book can be your step-by-step guide to identify, pursue, and secure your ideal career. The book is divided into three parts that represent the three major phases in the Nth Degree process: Discover, Define, and Drive. In the Discover phase, you'll identify where you are Now with foundational values and commitments, and you'll determine how you add value both through your Nature (the talents and personality you were born with) and your Nurture (the skills and knowledge you've developed over time). In the Define phase, you'll clarify your precise Niche—the genius zone you can uniquely offer to the marketplace that elevates you from employee to asset. Finally, in the Drive phase, you'll learn to Network strategically, Navigate like a pro, and Nourish your career journey as you experience a lifetime of career success.

Each chapter guides you through an important lesson within one of the seven steps of the Nth Degree strategy. At the end of each chapter, there is a short section titled Become Unstoppable with targeted action steps for you to apply the lessons in each chapter to your own life and career. Be sure to record your insights from these in a notebook or a digital document. If you want real transformation, don't just "think about it" and move on. The goal is to get everything out of your head so you can view it objectively and make the next best career decision with this new, clear information.

An Intro to the Nth Degree

To begin, let's get you familiar with the main steps of the Nth Degree framework.

As you can see from the diagram, the model is represented in a circular fashion. This shape is mean to symbolically suggest that the process is iterative and never-ending (yet another word beginning with the letter N!). Before you freak out, let me explain. The purpose of the process is to equip you with everything you need to know to make your next, best career decision. Despite our greatest efforts to control everything—including our professional destiny—life

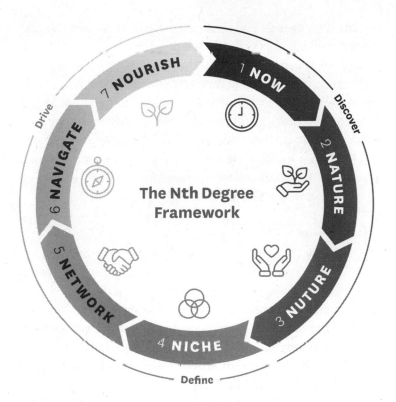

The Nth Degree Framework

DISCOVER	DEFINE	DRIVE
1 NOW Explore your current circumstances, core values, and commitments	**4 NICHE** Create your Olympic-gold-medal-level career sweet spot	**5 NETWORK** Strategically empower and leverage career advocates
2 NATURE Access your personality, behaviors, gifts, and aptitudes		**6 NAVIGATE** Test drive your career ideas before going all in
3 NUTURE Dive into your cumulative knowledge, skills, and expertise		**7 NOURISH** Commit to consistent reevaluation and career evolution

has its own agenda and rhythms. As you may have already experienced, just as you get used to a "new normal," life can throw unexpected situations at you that require you to pivot. You have three options in response to this reality: ignore the situation completely, fight it tooth and nail to maintain a semblance of control, or embrace the inevitability of change and plan for it. To do the latter, you'll need to practice a proven methodology to make the best decisions given your new and evolving circumstances. By learning the Nth Degree process for clarity, you will be equipped with such a strategy.

Step 1: Now

Regardless of where you are in life, you will always begin the Nth Degree process with Now. This starting point honors and acknowledges your current phase of life. Whether you've just graduated high school or you're considering your "encore career" in retirement, your phase of life largely dictates your current circumstances. By clearly acknowledging your current reality and set of responsibilities, you begin the process of self-discovery grounded in an objective understanding of your viable possibilities. Someone who's twenty-four, debt-free, rents an apartment, and doesn't even own a goldfish has a different set of circumstances and responsibilities than someone who is forty-two, married, has three children and two dogs, and owns a home. This isn't bad or good, better or worse—it just *is*. If you honor your reality, your Now, you can create a plan of action firmly rooted in viability and "grow where you are planted."

The first step, Now, also encompasses the values, commitments, and rules by which you live at that point in your life. As you can imagine, the single twenty-four-year-old and the married forty-two-year-old are likely to have different sets of core values and commitments along with their differing circumstances. Once again, one set isn't right, the other isn't wrong. These principles simply reflect the current states and phases of life. Understanding your own parameters and standards of living allows you to drill down into what really matters to you right now.

Steps 2 and 3: Nature and Nurture

Once you're clear on your circumstances, values, and commitments, you can move on to the next two core steps of the Discover phase of the Nth Degree: your Nature and your Nurture. Together, Nature and Nurture represent how we add value in the world, so these two elements can be thought of as the opposite sides of the same coin. One side is value that you give and display naturally and the other side is value that you've learned and developed over time. That first side of the coin, your Nature, is your personality and behaviors as well as your natural gifts and talents—that which comes easily to you and allows you to excel without much effort. To explore this side of your value coin, you'll complete a few assessments and leverage the "mirrors" that your network provides to you. The other side of the value coin, your Nurture, is the cumulative knowledge, skills, and expertise born of your collective experiences—your education, work history, extracurricular pursuits, hobbies, travel, and the like. To explore this side of the coin, you'll dive back into your previous work, education, and life experiences to determine what value you bring with you going forward.

Step 4: Niche

Once you've thoroughly uncovered all of the facts of your situation in the Discover phase—completing the steps of Now, Nature, and Nurture—you will move on to the Define phase in which there is only one major step: Niche. In the Nth Degree framework, the term Niche refers to your genius zone. You might think of it as your sandbox or your professional sweet spot. No matter what you call it, your Niche represents your best and highest professional value. By starting with your life principles (Now) and leveraging both your natural gifts (Nature) and learned talents (Nurture), you get a complete picture of your ideal career. Better yet, because no one in the world has the same combination of Now, Nature, and Nurture as you, your Niche is completely unique. When you identify it, what you define is the professional pursuit at which no one else can compete with you. This is also the place in which you give maximum value and from which you receive maximum fulfillment. When you can articulate this newly defined niche, you elevate yourself from generic employee to a singular and untouchable asset.

Is there anything better than that? Yes, there is. Turning that *vision* into your *reality*.

Steps 5, 6, and 7: Network, Navigate, and Nourish

Together, the three steps in the Drive phase of the methodology equip you to turn your vision into your professional reality. Knowing your Niche is great. Living it every single day is better. The three steps within the Drive phase—Network, Navigate, and Nourish—will help you realize (a.k.a. make real) your vision *faster*.

For most of us, "network" has become a dirty word: upon hearing it, we picture poorly lit conference rooms and slimy people handing out business cards. In the Nth Degree methodology, you will reclaim and redefine the word "network" so that it represents the most natural and easiest way to involve career advocates and professional sponsors in your search. In the Network step, you will learn to purposefully grow your network to facilitate your dream by properly leveraging the power of people.

Instead of going all in on a new job with only a hope and prayer that you'll like it, the proven strategies in Navigate force you to test your career assumptions before making bigger decisions. By placing little bets throughout your search process, you can inspect what you expect from any given job or role. Just as professional developers use design thinking to ideate, prototype, test, and iterate products, you will use similar strategies to prove the fit and viability of any career choice you consider. These tools cure any potentially reactionary behaviors ("*anywhere* is better than *here*") and set you up with a proven plan to secure the role of your dreams.

Last, but certainly not least, is Nourish. Once you've discovered your true professional value, defined your uniquely niched zone of genius, and begun your career search by leveraging people and investigation strategies, you'll be on the road to making your hard-fought vision into your reality. Yahtzee, right? Well, anyone who has been in a job search or a career transition knows that the process can be long, tedious, and demoralizing as you wade through a slew of ill-fitting job opportunities, less-than-optimal interviews, and last-minute corporate restructuring decisions. Even someone who's fastidiously completed the first six steps in the Nth Degree will be tempted at some point to throw up their hands and declare the process a failure. The purpose of Nourish is to equip you with a bank of motivation for when the going gets tough. You will learn the importance of having a purpose or a strong why behind your career pursuits, how to put that pursuit in the context of a life well lived, and how to summon courage and bravery when fear or doubt comes knocking.

Committing to the Process

When you reach this "final" phase, you're living the Nth Degree to its fullest extent. The only thing you'll have left to do is choose your next career step, sign on the dotted line, and start living up to your fullest professional potential. Before we begin with Now, I invite you to make this one commitment: *trust in the process*. No more reactionary decisions. No more out-of-the-frying-pan-into-the-fire choices. No more wondering if the grass is greener. Instead, lean in to a step-by-step process for career clarity that is proven to work. Let this time through the Nth Degree be but the first of many amazing career decisions. After your initial time through the methodology, you will have a practiced methodology ready for when your circumstances change; you'll always be prepared to make the next best decision for your ideal career—and ultimately for your ideal life.

PART ONE

DISCOVER

"Setting goals is the first step in turning the invisible into the visible."

TONY ROBBINS

1

GET YOUR MIND RIGHT

HAVE A FRIEND from college who is notorious for asking bold questions and expecting immediate answers. She has no filter and no shame. If she wants to know your salary, she'll ask. If she wants to discuss politics with her new boyfriend's parents, she'll do it. And if she is feeling philosophical, she'll corner you and make you analyze the deepest parts of your soul that you've (likely) been ignoring. Some of her absolute favorites (and consequently the most infuriating) were questions about the future. The one that would simultaneously peak my anger and stir the initial stages of a panic attack for me was this: "If money were no object and you could have any job you wanted, what would it be?"

Cue part befuddled, part furious, part deer-in-headlights Tracy face. First of all, this question gave me an insane amount of anxiety. I had no idea what I wanted to be "when I grew up," let alone what I would do if I could do *anything*. And in what universe would money not matter?! How was I supposed to access a world of pure imagination and possibility when I knew I would have bills to pay and have at least one mouth to feed?

Two words: red wine.

One day, many years after the first time she posed that infernal question to me, we were catching up over a couple glasses of merlot at her apartment in D.C. Her career had been progressing rapidly while mine was, well, DOA. I had just quit my six-figure job on the trading floor (some might call this a strong reaction to a quarter-life crisis), and I had committed to enrolling in Semester at Sea—an undergraduate study-abroad program that houses students on a large ship and sails them around the world. Everything I owned was in storage. I was paying for the trip in installments, which would ultimately use every last bit of my savings. And most terrifyingly of all, I had no idea what I wanted to do with my life.

Semester at Sea was my last-ditch, all-in effort to figure myself out. Thus, for her, the perfect time for soul-probing. "Okay, now that you're out of the bank, I want you to answer my question. If money were no object and you could have any job you wanted, what would it be?" Once I retracted the daggers I'd shot from my eyes, I lifted my glass and finished my drink. Taking a deep breath and fighting the urge to blow the question off completely, I thought about it: "What *would* I do, if I could do anything . . . ?" And then it hit me. I no longer had anything to lose. I was already unemployed and living off my savings. Why not give it a go?

I looked her in the eyes and the words just started spilling out. "Honestly, I'd do exactly what we're doing right now. I would sit with people—friends, family, colleagues, strangers—and we'd have a drink—water, coffee, or wine. And I would just *talk about life*. I'd ask them about their pursuits and their dreams. I'd delve into their stories, their families, their lives. I would just talk to people and see if I could provide any valuable insight or at least allow them to feel heard. Yep. I'd do *that*."

In that moment, I didn't think anything of my answer. After all, this wasn't a revelation. If you've known me for five minutes, you know I love red wine. Even sooner than that, you know that I love people and I find their stories and their lives infinitely fascinating. My favorite "hobby" has always been spending time with my friends and catching up about our lives. Connecting. Creating community. Learning from each other. Supporting one another. I've had an obsession with the inner workings of the human mind and our seemingly irrational behaviors ever since I can remember. I just never thought it was anything special. Most importantly for this context, I certainly didn't think it was a *career*. Boy, was I wrong!

Fast-forward five years, almost to the day of that conversation, and where was I? Sitting in my office's coworking space, talking to a brand-new coaching client. It was the first day of our coaching engagement, so we were knee-deep in the Discover phase—going over everything he could remember about his life and his current set of circumstances, mining it for patterns and information that could help us in his search for his ideal career. As he talked, I listened and typed furiously while taking occasional sips of my black coffee. The hour went by in what seemed like minutes, and at the end of the session, as I packed up my computer, I had one of those slow-motion movie moments. "Whoa," I thought. "I'm *actually* doing it." I realized that one of the basic functions of my job was exactly what I had answered five years prior to my friend's question of what my ideal would be—I was having a drink, listening to someone's story, and trying to help.

And here's the best part: I was getting paid!

Between leaving my job in finance and starting my own business, I had many experiences that led me to what I do today. But perhaps the most important thing that changed during that period of self-discovery was my mindset. What I said I would do if money were no object sounded like a hobby

Only when an idea is available to you and **you believe it is a *possibility* can you make it a *reality*.**

or a pastime; I never once considered the idea that my red-wine-infused musing would be my job. Not only that but a *career* that paid. Work that I love doing. That I am good at doing. That brings meaning to my life and impact to the world. But that's exactly what it ended up being because of my shift in mindset.

My dream literally became my reality. I owe that to my friend's challenging question. And, of course, to red wine. But most importantly, to the significant shift in my mindset that took place over the two years after I left my job in finance.

Creating a Possibility Mindset

Allow me to explain this concept. Sure, when I imagined a life where money was no object and my choices had no consequences, I could see myself drinking wine and gossiping all day long. In particular, I pictured that happening in Italy! But the shift from daydreaming about what an independently wealthy and Italian-speaking version of Tracy would do to centering my professional pursuits on this vision did not happen overnight. Until I became aware of a role that required those specific behaviors and understood that I could monetize those activities, I couldn't believe it was viable possibility for me. They say you can't know what you don't know. When you lack exposure to the reality of an idea, it remains just that—an idea. A "must be nice." A dream. When I didn't readily see my vision as a profession, I believed my idea was limited to the realm of imagination rather than a possible reality.

However, just as a brain will struggle to see a possibility of which it is not aware, so too will the brain focus on something that it holds top of mind. Maybe you've heard of this

before—psychologists call it the Baader-Meinhof phenomenon, but it's more commonly known as the frequency illusion.
Here's an easy example. Imagine that you're out shopping
for a car. After an arduous day of visiting multiple dealer-
ships, you finally find it—the ideal, unique, personalized car
of your dreams. It's the perfect color, the perfect size. Better
still, it's the perfect price. You decide to spend your hard-
earned money on this baby, take it home, and sleep soundly
that night with the comfort and satisfaction of a decision well
made.

The next day, you take your sweet new ride out for a spin.
You just know that you're going to impress and everyone will
be blown away by your unique new wheels. Then suddenly
you realize (in horror) that your new ride is everywhere! Every
one of your neighbors has the same car. You see two more of
them when you get stuck in traffic later that day. While you're
watching TV that night, there's a commercial for the same car,
which, interestingly enough, you hadn't ever seen before you
bought it! And it's the exact same color.

The frequency illusion happens all the time but we rarely
notice, or we explain it away as coincidence or luck. The
Baader-Meinhof phenomenon explains why something
you've only just noticed, experienced, or been told about
suddenly seems to be everywhere. From your perspective,
what you see seems to be appearing more frequently than it
was before. In reality, it was always there, so that's an illusion.
You're simply *noticing* it more than you did before because
now it's top of mind.

In your career, this phenomenon has significant impli-
cations: until an idea is firmly imprinted in your brain, you
believe in its reality, and you allow yourself to see it as a
possibility, you will never *really notice* opportunities to do
it. That means your dream job could be right in front of you,
and you could be missing it. In fact, you are missing it. Our

brains focus on perceiving what we already believe, which is why limiting beliefs about your version of reality can have a powerful hold over your life. If you believe in something negative—such as the notion that work has to be hard, you have to be miserable to make a lot of money, or you're not qualified for what you want to do—then you will only *see* a reality that further proves you to be right. You will perceive the world in a way that confirms your beliefs and takes you further and further away from the possibility of your dreams.

So, the first hurdle you have to overcome is your current perception of reality. No big deal, right? While that might sound daunting, all that is required of you is to start challenging that ingrained mindset that what you *know* is all that there *is*. As you can imagine, this is not easy at first, but like meditation, it gets easier over time. Changing how you perceive reality involves a certain unlearning process. But once you achieve this shift in mindset, not only can you surmount the limiting beliefs and the inane self-inflicted expectations that are keeping you stuck, but you can also continually monitor for negative self-fulfilling prophesies, thoughts, and behaviors along the road to sustainable success.

At this point, you probably don't know exactly what you want to do. And that's okay! That's why you're reading this book. If you don't have your ideal career in your mind's eye right now, that doesn't mean your ideal career does not exist or will never become your reality. The key is to start opening your mind to the *possibility* of perceiving your career and life differently. As you move through the Nth Degree career clarity process, you are going to fill that open mind with opportunities that you'll need to believe in before you can see them.

And with that new set of opportunities comes new and different choices. How do you make the best choices? By embracing the idea of regret-free living.

Regret-Free Living

In life, we have a lot of decisions to make. Some decisions are small (PB&J or a BLT?). Some decisions are large (corporate or entrepreneur?). So, how do you know if you're making the right decision or a decision that will ultimately result in regret? Without fail, every single person whom I've had the honor to enroll in our programs has shared this exact same worry. This fear of being wrong creates decision-making paralysis. In the absence of a strategy to overcome fear, our lives and careers become stagnant as our agency and sense of control withers. But thankfully, for you and me, I have learned a little something about regret-free living that I hope will free you from the prison of your own fears.

Here's the lowdown: modern psychology breaks down regrets into two categories. You can experience regrets of commission, which means to regret something you did, or regrets of omission, which means to regret something you did not do.

Regrets of commission are understandably painful. You do something wrong. You find out, get found out, or come to terms with the fact that you did something wrong. You endure some type of consequence. You experience regret and (hopefully) repentance for what you did wrong. And the experience is over. Done. Dusted. On to the next. This sort of cycle happens all the time when people make what they deem to be bad decisions. The process usually follows the same predictable stages: you decide, take action, get punished, regret what you did, and move on.

These kinds of regrets all share that similar closed-loop structure—a beginning, middle, and end. Yes, the outcome often sucks. That's part of regret. But at the end of the day, there is a resolution you can (eventually) reconcile. Acceptance and reconciliation may be difficult, but they are possible.

And it's precisely that possibility that distinguishes between these two types of regrets.

The second type of regret is impossible to forget because it inherently lacks resolution. Regrets of omission—regret for things you did not do—have no final or tangible outcome. No consequence. Or so it seems... More accurately, they have an *infinite* number of possible outcomes or potential resolutions. It is precisely this uncertainty—the unanswerable what-ifs—that elevates this type of regret over the other. The brain loves closed loops. Regret without resolution can haunt you for a lifetime, simply because of the lack of clear resolution. In the absence of a known outcome, the brain continues to fruitlessly search for one. In search of resolution, your mind clings to all the different possibilities, so you regret what you omitted not just once but over and over and over again.

By letting fear of an outcome that you can't predict guide your decision-making, you'll take the exact route through life that produces *more* regrets, not fewer. You may feel as though you're protecting yourself from the regret of career failure by playing it safe. But choosing *not to try* opens you up to a cycle of regrets that could go on forever.

I ask that as you progress through this process, you embrace this lesson as it pertains to your career. Take your meaningful shot at the stars, whatever that may be. Fear, the most primal and visceral hurdle, keeps us from finding meaningful, fulfilling work. Everyone's fear base is different, but the result is the same. Lifelong, crippling regret about the things we never did, and how we wish we had been brave enough to try. Don't let this happen to you. Take your shot, knowing that even if you fail, you'll never regret the failure more than not trying at all.

Paralysis by analysis, or the art of not deciding, is a choice in and of itself. It's also a habit that many find challenging to break. To begin shifting this mindset, I offer you a couple of tips. First, make a what-if list. Think back on your major life decisions: relationships you started or ended, conversations that did or didn't take place, places you did or didn't move to, communities you got involved with or left, and so on. Which what-ifs still remain? What do you wish you knew the answer to? What do you struggle to let go of when you're falling asleep at night? The angst this list creates will likely be enough to encourage you to make proactive decisions going forward and provide some incredibly powerful motivation. Practice your new decisive mindset by committing to newer, stronger, forward-focused decision-making.

Another trick, and my personal favorite, is to imagine yourself in your twilight years. The next time you have a decision to make, imagine yourself as an elderly person looking back on your life. When I do this, I'm ninety-plus years old, sitting on a porch in a rocking chair, with an afghan draped over my shoulders and a cat sitting quietly in my lap. I ask that version of myself, "Will I regret this decision?" or "Will I regret not doing this?" I'm proud to report that Granny Tracy has been right 100 percent of the time.

Purpose versus Passion

"What is your passion?" No other sentence in the English language has caused me as much angst and anxiety as this four-word question. For the longest time, I tried to ignore it, but that damn thing is everywhere! College admissions essays, job interviews, red-wine-induced existential conversations... you simply can't escape it. At one point, I was so consumed by my lack of a clear passion that I made it my mission, nay, my quest, to find it. I joined passion clubs. I read self-help blogs. I bought books. I took tests. I even went so far as to track down my high school guidance counselor to see what I could learn from her. But the truth kept staring me directly in the face: I had no idea—zero, zip, zilch, nada—what my passion might be.

Even when I started my coaching business, which felt both personally meaningful and purposeful, I still struggled with how to articulate one singular passion. To make matters more complicated, I had to deal with clients who were struggling with the exact same confusing idea—this elusive concept of "knowing your passion." They looked to me to fill that ever-present void that came from their lack of clarity. Of course, that disconnect left me feeling like a fraud in my own area of expertise.

One day, three years into my coaching business, I was given a gift that alleviated this anxiety. A life-changing counselor taught me a lesson that reframed my epic search for my passion, and it has served me beautifully ever since. At a counseling session, I shared with my therapist that I'd had a breakthrough in my professional messaging. For the longest time I'd been searching for my core message, and that day I was happy to say that I had found it. Naturally, she was intrigued, so I pulled out my notebook, cleared my throat, prepared for the fanfare that awaited me. I said, "I help people figure out what they were *created to do*." I paused and waited for the inevitable round of applause and tearful excitement. Nothing happened. So, I put it a different way. "You know, it all comes down to identifying and doing that which we were created for . . . what we're meant to be. That's what a passion really is! That's what my message is going to be."

Her response: pause . . . head tilt . . . brow furrow . . . sigh.

"You don't like it, do you?" I said, without hiding my disappointment.

"It's not that," she said. "It's just not true. We don't have one passion for which we were created."

To really comprehend the stunned look on my face, you have to know that my counselor ran a Christian-based therapy practice. We started every session with a prayer about God's will. Of all the people on the planet, I thought she would be supportive of the idea of being created for a reason. So, after I finally picked up my jaw from the floor and convinced my ego not to flee the room, I somehow found the courage to ask her why.

"We weren't created for just *one* thing," she said. "No one has only one passion or purpose. We have many. And they are constantly changing."

Her answer was equally stunning. I'm sorry, what?! What about all those passion clubs and personality tests and miserable freakin' essay questions that demand to know our one, singular, easy-to-articulate passion? What gives!

"Take, for instance, what's going on in my life. I'm a professional counselor running my own practice. I do speaking engagements, panels, and facilitations. I'm a wife and mother of two grown women. I'm a grandmother. I volunteer. But let's put that all aside for a moment. Right now, my youngest daughter is preparing to be married. That makes me mother of the bride. I feel, deep down, that right now my passion, my purpose, is to be the best mother of the bride I can possibly be.

"So, what does that mean?" she continued. "I'm not taking extra speaking gigs. I'm not taking on any new clients. I've scaled back my volunteering. Every bit of my spare time is dedicated to figuring out how I can be a better mother of the bride. And that's all well and good ... for now. But at some point, if all goes to plan, my daughter is going to get married. And then what? I'm no longer going to be mother of the bride. So, if I've defined that as my one passion, one purpose, and one destiny and then it ends, *what happens next?*"

This idea was so logical, so common sense that I almost beat myself up for not seeing it sooner. No wonder we've all been frustrated, anxious, and miserable trying to define our passion or discover our purpose. It's an insanely misguided. exercise! Trying to choose a singular passion or purpose means we have to actively ignore the only consistency in life: *change*. Maybe instead of forcing a passion epiphany we should be asking, What is my passion *right now*? What is my purpose *at this phase of life*? What is my destiny *today*?

That day in her office, with my ego deflated but my mind open to a new reality, I first conceived of the Nth Degree being an iterative model designed for change. Not just a one-time career breakthrough but a concept that could be used repeatedly as our lives and circumstances evolve. So, whether this is your first time or your fiftieth time going through the Nth Degree methodology, begin at the beginning: the Discover phase and its very first step, Now.

BECOME UNSTOPPABLE: YOUR NEW OPEN MINDSET

Step 1: Know that a mindset is not one size fits all.
Creating a possibility mindset is not a one-time exercise or a one-size-fits-all endeavor. Some people have an epiphany reading the preceding paragraphs. Others have to meditate on and practice this idea for weeks or months for it to really sink in. For those of you who are still seeking inspiration, what follows are a few suggestions to practice an open mindset and see more possibility in your life.

Step 2: Write and repeat a daily affirmation.

On the background of my computer is an image of a man riding a bicycle with a woman riding on the handlebars with the following affirmation:

> I expand myself in abundance, success, and love every day in every way.
> So I'm open to receiving all that I seek.
> So I can inspire others to do the same.
> With God as my strength.

I read that affirmation to myself every day and I keep it on my computer to remind me to do so. If you don't have an affirmation of your own, borrow mine. If you have other words you prefer, go to town. Either way, keep your affirmation close to you and repeat it often. What we think, we become.

Step 3: Begin or continue a meditation practice.

Meditation used to scare the crap out of me. I was Julia Roberts's character in *Eat Pray Love*—I could barely be silent for five minutes let alone sit still for a meditation. But by using apps like Headspace and Calm, I began a brief and infrequent practice of meditation that has served me greatly when I am practicing and leaves a significant hole when I am not. There are a ton of meditation resources online, many of which are great for beginners. Find a recording or use an app to build a practice of being mindful, which will help you envision possibility in your life.

Step 4: Explore hypnotherapy.

Okay, hear me out. Hypnotherapy does not mean clucking like a chicken on a stage in Vegas. Before I tried it, I thought that's what it was, and you might too. A few years ago, when I joined a professional mastermind, one of the benefits was a monthly meeting with a hypnotherapist. I drummed up a little courage to try something new, and I can now say without a doubt that this man and his strategies have made the single largest contribution to the improvement in my mindset to date. Don't knock it till you try it. To find a solid resource near you, begin by asking friends and mentors you trust for recommendations. If that proves fruitless, start by doing local searches online and make sure to check reviews.

"Grow where you are planted."

PROVERB

2

THE ONLY LOGICAL
PLACE TO START

WHAT DOES IT mean to start with now? It may be tempting to think that focusing on the current state of your life is not the best first step to creating an ideal future. This concern is especially true for those of us who are struggling in miserable careers. If you have a soul-crushing job that leaves you drained at the end of the day, why focus on that? Why not start by envisioning and planning for the future? But the reality is this: now—where you are in your life right at this moment—is the only place you *can* start.

Getting where you want to go has to start with moving from where you are right now. Taking stock of where you are now allows you to use your current situation as a foundation from which you can build. This practice also allows you to avoid repeating your past mistakes. Ever heard the proverb "grow where you are planted"? It means that in order to get to the bigger and better version of you, you must first outgrow wherever you are. Successfully moving on requires that you get everything you can out of your current circumstances. When you don't take the time to learn from your past or take stock of your present, you risk repeating the same mistakes in the future or forcing yourself into a new reality for which you are not ready.

For example, have you ever felt like you're in a weird cycle of loving your job for the first few months only to find that when you've achieved some minor level of mastery you get bored and want to move on? Or do you keep getting the same nagging piece of advice, feedback, or criticism from your boss, no matter what job you're in? What about that one annoying type of person who seems to be at every company you work for? You are not imagining this. It's really happening. But not because all jobs get boring eventually or no boss will ever understand you or every job has that one annoying dude. These circumstances keep repeating themselves because of *you*. You are the only constant in each of these scenarios. So, if something keeps happening to you, it's a major sign that you've got a pattern begging to be addressed.

Starting with where you are creates a launch pad to your future. Choosing instead to jump from problem (I hate my job) to solution (get a new job) is what we like to call a reactionary decision. At best, you put a bandage on a bigger problem. Maybe life gets a little better, but it's still not your best. At worst, you fool yourself into thinking you'll be happier once you're at that new job, only to find the exact same frustrations you were trying to escape! You fall back into the exact same patterns. (Hello, boredom, crappy bosses, and annoying colleagues.) Instead, by taking a strong look at where you are and then using that information to get to where you want to go, you move forward with clear intention.

If you're in a tough spot right now, you might be thinking about how stuck you feel and how few options you have. That's completely normal and natural—I went through it too! But, trust me, the best way to move forward is to appreciate where you are currently and take your next steps with that knowledge in mind. If you look at your circumstances with a little objectivity, you might discover more opportunities than you first perceived. Every step in life prepares you for the next.

Recognize what you have now and use it to get to where you want to go.

My job is to help you discover and leverage that truth in your life *right now*.

When you feel stuck—truly, awfully stuck—the only way to become unstuck is to challenge your perception. You'll need to view your circumstances in a different way—with more objectivity, in particular. Adding a little objectivity to the mix allows you to see your situation with more clarity. You know how you can always see a clear answer when your friend comes to you with a problem, but when you're faced with the same dilemma, a solution seems impossible? Objectivity—a difference in perspective—is the mechanism at play. You're never as stuck as you feel. Getting unstuck means letting go: of expectations, of fear, and of the perceived security that's keeping you from seeing (and taking advantage of) all your other options. In order to make this mental shift in perception, you'll need a logical way to achieve a different perspective.

Shift Your Perspective: The Eight-Part Life Audit

The first exercise in the Now step of the Nth Degree is a comprehensive life audit to get crystal clear on everything going on in your life right now. By doing this exercise first, you create a foundational place from which to grow. You also allow yourself to move forward with specific, dynamic ideas for the future.

As complex as our lives might be, they can be broken down into a relatively small set of categories. After years of work in this area, I've identified eight major categories that comprise the majority of the who, what, when, where, why, and how of our everyday lives. I recommend going one by one through each of them and methodically examining where you are in this moment, in this phase of life. Not where you *want* to be or *wish* you were but where you *are* right now. The categories are as follows:

Emotional
Environmental
Financial
Intellectual
Physical
Professional
Social
Spiritual

As much as possible, avoid the temptation to get stuck in the audit process. The goal here is to take stock of the current state of affairs rather than live in or complain about the past. The idea of a life audit may also feel dauting and pointless: "Work sucks, my friends are tired of me complaining about it, and even my cat knows I'm miserable. Audit complete." While the exercise may seem fruitless at first, an objective life audit will actually uncover components of your life you may have overlooked or underappreciated. Every one of my previous clients has learned that their circumstances allowed for much more latitude and possibility than they ever imagined. Slowly but surely, the feeling of being stuck will be replaced with a solid foundation and a present and a clear vision for the future.

A Peek into My First Life Audit

I'll prove it to you. My very first life audit, back in 2012, was an eye-opening experience to say the least. Before I forced myself to be objective and comprehensive with my audit, I thought my life was in ruins. The job that I hated had so permeated my thoughts that everything else felt miserable right along with it. After I did this audit, I came to a strange realization: I had far more going for me than I first perceived. Here's the CliffsNotes version of how that went:

Emotional: Dead inside. Work is sucking my soul. Next.

Environmental: Awesome roommate. Renting. Within running distance to the water. Forty-five-minute train to New York City. Nothing tying me down.

Financial: Without realizing it, and likely because I was raised by a very risk-averse mom, I have squirreled away ten months' worth of expenses in my emergency fund. Feels like finding a $20 bill in my coat pocket, only better. Yahtzee!

Intellectual: What? Next.

Physical: If I weren't going to CrossFit daily, I'd weigh about 100 extra pounds with all the wine and food I'm consuming.

Professional: In a word? Miserable. Next.

Social: Single. Friends are super-tired of me complaining. My parents love and support me, but their advice sucks right now.

Spiritual: Despite questioning the very nature of life itself, I still dutifully go to church every Sunday and confession once a month.

When I took a step back, I realized three very important things:

1 My social circle provided an incredible support system.
2 My financial situation afforded me more options than I had expected.
3 My lack of long-term attachments meant I had some freedom to explore.

I didn't need to jump to another potentially miserable job right away. I wasn't nearly as stuck as I had thought.

That is the big idea behind this audit: getting you to feel less stuck. When you see all the components of your life, not just the professional realm, you can remind yourself that you have more going for you than your (miserable) job! With that knowledge in mind, you start to dig yourself out of the "I don't know" hole, so you can finally answer that always-terrifying question, "What the heck do I want to do with my life?" Once you're done with your life audit, you're going to have a ton of new information that's finally out of your head and on paper. This will be a liberating experience.

Overcoming the Inevitable Objection

"But, Tracy," you ask, "what if my situation is truly dire and there's no hope for me? I don't have a fat savings account or a spouse to support me. Has this ever *not* worked?" My response: no. This exercise works. Please do the audit, even if your situation seems hopeless. If you do this honestly and objectively, like my client Steve did, you'll find the silver linings. When we started working together, Steve was in a bad way—he was a father to a one-year-old and estranged from the child's mother. He had moved home to help care for his elderly parents. He had recently shut down a business he'd been running for ten years. In his own words, he was slowly crawling into debt and depression.

I'll admit I was worried when it came to Steve's life audit exercise. Would he be the first person for whom the audit failed to produce a silver lining? Thankfully, the tried-and-true life audit worked its magic and delivered insights that he never expected. Steve found he could draw support from his environment, which provided diverse opportunities for work and companionship with like-minded people. He had an incredibly engaged family, a top-notch education, and a large capacity for intellectual growth. Finally, he had negotiated joint custody of his child, so he could balance parenting with full-time work. I was so impressed with his ability to identify the silver lining and draw on it for motivation. I'm sure you can do the same thing too.

The life audit is a powerful reframe, which is why it's the very first step on your journey from stuck to unstoppable.

BECOME UNSTOPPABLE:
YOUR CURRENT LIFE AUDIT

Step 1: Write down the eight major categories of your life.

Using one page per word in a notebook or a digital document, write down each of the eight categories that comprise your life:

Emotional

Environmental

Financial

Intellectual

Physical

Professional

Social

Spiritual

Set a timer for five minutes, and during that five minutes, jot down what immediately comes to mind when you think about the first category. Repeat for each category. Remember to do your best to complete this exercise without judgment. There are parts of your life that you'd like to improve, but that is not the purpose of this exercise. Instead, remain objective and write down as much as you can.

Step 2: Take a break.

Go for a walk. Have some coffee. Take a nap. Whatever you need to do to clear your head. You want to get away from the exercise long enough to clear your vision to see anything you might have missed. Take at least twenty minutes away from your notes, and do something that gets your heart rate up or creates clarity in your mind.

Step 3: Return to the audit and objectively review it.

I like to divide my insights in each category into two sections: what's going well and what could improve. The purpose here is to gain objectivity and identify the parts of your life you may be overlooking because of the areas that may feel overwhelming. Write down anything else that comes to mind, and be as objective as possible to create a comprehensive life audit.

Step 4: Take stock.

Review what you've written and draw some conclusions. Note the three to five components of your life or circumstances that feel the best and that you can use as your foundation going forward. Don't skip this. These foundational components will sustain you as you progress. Record these somewhere you can see them every day; I put mine on the mirror.

"Your beliefs become your thoughts. Your thoughts become your words. Your words become your actions. Your actions become your habits. Your habits become your values. Your values become your destiny."

MAHATMA GANDHI

3

WHAT REALLY
MATTERS TO YOU

A FEW YEARS AGO, I attended a networking event
by Young Catholic Professionals. The meeting fea-
tured an executive speaker, who shared his insights
on integrating faith into work and life. I had been to a few
of these before, so I was expecting the usual career story
sprinkled with tips and tricks for living a "good life." What I
got instead was a glimpse inside the mind of the most habit-
driven, self-disciplined person I have ever met. He shared
with us a step-by-step, foolproof, no-nonsense plan for
accomplishing your goals and making strong life decisions.
This man, Russell Huber, was no joke. He had a spreadsheet
for everything! I mean *everything*. He found that relying on his
own will or memory was too inconsistent (and stressful!), so
to complete the daily routines he believed led to "living his
best life," he wrote down every task and then checked items
off his list every day. *Every* day!

When he showed us his morning list, I knew the man was
for real (parenthetical comments are my reactions):

Wake up at five a.m. [Woof!]
Drink two full glasses of water and eat two carrots. [Umm,
that's awfully specific.]

Put on your workout clothes. [Did that really need to be written down?]
Tell yourself, "I like to work out. I want to work out."
[Bahahahaha!]
Stretch program. [Wow, this list is thorough...]
Exercise for thirty minutes. [Eureka! It all makes sense!][1]

His system is so simple. So effective! He doesn't have to remember *anything*. He doesn't have to "motivate himself" (unless it was built into his plan, of course). He doesn't have any excuses. He just reads his spreadsheet and does exactly what it says. Goals: boom, roasted.

Huber's basic argument is that all our behaviors, even the tiny and seemingly insignificant ones, determine what becomes of us and our lives. So, if you want to live a certain kind of life, you execute a certain set of behaviors. Simple. Naturally, my next questions were "How do you choose those behaviors? How do you know what kind of life?" Luckily, he had answers for those as well: let your values be your guide.

Core Values and Life's Decisions

The idea of core values might bring to mind a company's vision and mission statement or a presidential candidate's stump speech: cheesy, unnecessary, and, quite often, cosmetic. Before hearing Huber speak, I had never considered having personal core values—ones that were well-thought-out, written down, and committed to in a meaningful way. But after listening to his compelling talk, I realized something important: if you don't know your core values, a.k.a. what *really* matters to you, then what's driving your decisions? Further than that, how do you know if you've ever made a *good* decision?

Imagine defining a set of core values—in advance—against which you could measure any opportunity that comes your way. Instead of agonizing over the decision for days or weeks, you would know if the opportunity meets your predetermined criteria almost immediately. No unnecessary worrying. No lost sleep. Decision made! How much easier would those choices be? How much faster would you be able to get to the life you want? How much less stress and anxiety would you feel each day?

Here's the real deal: you're *already* operating with a set of personal core values. Each decision you make reflects those values. Every activity you do, every place you spend your time, every item on which you spend your money, every person you choose to interact with, every choice you make... reflects something you believe in or value. Otherwise, you wouldn't make that choice! All too often, we dismiss this truth because of cognitive dissonance. We explain away our choices as "out of our hands." The truth is your actions and choices are physical representations of your values. Have you defined your values or have your various choices? By reading this book, you're claiming that you're ready to do life differently and move your career forward intentionally. First, you need to identify your set of values to begin this journey.

Appreciating the Evolution of Values

Let's first get one thing clear: core values change throughout your life. That's right! You're not Moses. You're not writing these bad boys in stone. Remember, the only constant in life is change. Our circumstances are constantly evolving, so it follows that your set of core values will evolve as well. It's great to plan for the future, but honor the fact that what matters to you will be different even a year from now. Don't get tripped up by needing these values to be perfect or eternal. They can't be! No one set of values lasts forever. What matters is that these values are true for you in this moment. That's it.

When defining your core values for the first time, start by looking at your current circumstances and your background. Your behavior largely reflects your core values, whether or not they are well-thought-out. Where you go, who you're with, what you buy, and how you spend your time all say something about what matters to you. The idea here is to learn from your history, both what makes you proud and what you wish you could forget, to determine what your core values are right now.

As you go through this exercise, you might feel a little anxious. I know I did! Your life might not look the way you wish it did. In fact, it might not reflect any of your real core values at all. That was true for me when I first did this exercise. It's also been true for every single client I've had the privilege to serve. Some of your core values will be more aspirational than they are actual. If you're unhappy with your career or another key component of your life, it's most likely because you're living out of alignment with your core—with what truly matters to you.

A recent client, Jeremy, did this exercise and realized he was so unhappy with his job because of where he had to live in order to do it. He and his wife loved the mountains and being outside, and they wanted their two young children to grow up experiencing nature the way they had. But Jeremy's job in construction had led their family to settle in San Antonio, where they were suffering through 100-plus-degree summers with only molehills to speak of as mountains. When he wrote out his core values, he realized that the first step in getting his career on track was moving to a part of the country where his

If you're unhappy with your career, it's most likely because **you're living out of alignment with your core values.**

growing family could live in joy by experiencing nature and spending time outdoors. What began as a complaint about his job turned out to be a mismatch in location based on core values.

Your Yardstick for Decisions

Jeremy's results are not extraordinary—they're typical. These types of insights happen all the time. So, stop beating yourself up for things you've done in the past. The most successful people learn from their experiences and don't make the same mistake twice. A well-defined set of core values will begin to set the tone for your life and your career going forward.

If you do this process well, your core values will become the essence of your personal identity. They will reflect your principles, beliefs, and philosophies about life. And if you use them correctly, they will guide your decisions, no matter the external circumstances. If you feel like a failure at your job, if your mom keeps bothering you about getting married (just me?), or if you're craving children but haven't had them yet— you can look to your core values to remind yourself of who you are, where you are, and what *really* matters to you.

The process that I teach for creating a set of core values is simple. It includes five basic steps to take you from all the values in the world—freedom, authenticity, collaboration, stability, adventure, discipline, and so many more—to your personally tailored core set. Give yourself about an hour to complete this exercise. And remember you only cheat yourself by not being honest here. Own where you are in your life right now, and get clear on what really matters to you. Only then can you hope to live a life and career that you truly enjoy.

BECOME UNSTOPPABLE:
FIVE STEPS TO YOUR CORE VALUES

Step 1: Clear your mind of assumptions.

A beginner approaches a new subject with an open mind that sees many different possibilities. Adopt a beginner's mindset and forget everything you think you know. Keep an attitude of openness, eagerness, and lack of preconceptions when studying the subject of yourself. As you start this process, try to forget all the assumptions you have about success and what makes a good life. Be honest with yourself about what really matters to *you*, not to your friends, your family, or your coworkers. A beginner's mindset will help you see connections and opportunities you never would have otherwise. I do this exercise once per year, and each time I force myself to begin anew and don't look at my previous year's core values until after I've completed my new list.

Step 2: Do a ten-twenty-thirty brainstorm.

This step is three in one—you brainstorm for ten, then twenty, and finally thirty minutes to generate and refine your core values. Use a notebook, a sheet of paper, or a digital document (I prefer a spreadsheet!) to record your brainstorming.

For the first ten minutes, write down everything that comes to mind when you think about your core values. *Ev-er-y-thiiing.* Look over your life audit and think about your background. What brings you joy? When do you feel in a flow state? What matters to you most in the world? Everything that matters to you. Write it down. There is no right or wrong in the ten-minute brainstorm. These values can be in the form of whatever comes to mind: words, phrases, pictures, scenarios, you name it! Don't limit yourself. Be free!

For the next twenty minutes, add values to your ten-minute brainstorm list by referring to a preexisting list of core values. A quick Google search will yield many lists of core values, with words like adventure, creativity, leadership, freedom, love, optimism, and so on. Choose one with at least 100 entries. Yes, I know reading through a list of core values sounds tedious. But you cannot skip this! By mindfully searching such a list, you will discover values you really care about that didn't pop into your head earlier. Every time I do this, I find new words that resonate with me, and it helps me see how my values evolve year over year. Once completed, you will have pages (or a spreadsheet!) full of values-based words and ideas. Now you're ready for...

The final thirty-minute step. The goal here is to look at your words and phrases and start identifying patterns or groups. As you notice two words or phrases that describe the same value to you, create your first group. Review all the words you've recorded and don't stop until each one is categorized. For example, if you wrote down family, friends, solid coworkers, church-goers, and happy relationships, you might group those together because they all relate to community. By placing similar ideas together, you get to the real core of what matters to you.

Step 3: Give your values inspiring names.

Consider your groups of values. For each group, what one word or phrase encapsulates the whole? Or what one person or character defines this value for you? Give each group of aligned values a name that *inspires* you. For instance, if you wrote down good health, overall wellness, physical fitness, mental challenges, and working out, then you might call that group "health and wellness" and that would be fine. But how much more inspiring would that value be if you called it "feeling like a million bucks" or "badassery"? Don't overlook the power of language here. Core values resonate and operate at a higher level when they are defined in a meaningful way.

You can absolutely keep it simple. But sometimes a little creativity keeps the inspiration flame flickering. One year, one of my core values was "Braveheart" and I kept a picture of Mel Gibson's painted face next to my list. You better believe whenever my freedom came into question, I was not going to back down.

When you're done with this step, you will have narrowed your brainstormed list of core values down to a manageable number. The majority of my clients end up with somewhere between seven and ten values. Don't stress about having a pretty, round number. Eight well-thought-out core values beat ten half-assed values any day of the week.

Step 4: Nap it out.

Yep. Perhaps my favorite step. Take a nap (or a longer snooze) and see how you feel afterward. Science shows that while we're sleeping, our brains integrate information and store it for long-term use. In college, I used this to my advantage. Even if I had stayed up until three a.m. studying for an eight a.m. test, I would sleep for a few hours, because I knew that my brain needed time to digest the information I had stuffed inside it. Nine times out of ten, my recall the next day (a.k.a. the *same* day) was significantly better because of it.

If the values you chose are truly yours, you should have a pretty good reaction to them upon waking. Thinking about them should be satisfying or even make you smile. If they don't inspire you and you can't see yourself making decisions around them, then perhaps those values aren't really that important. If this is the case, go back to step 1.

Step 5: Ruthlessly order and test, test, test.

Once you've brain-dumped, grouped, named, and napped out your values, it's time to test them. Your core values will guide your decisions going forward. You can test each of them by asking yourself serious questions about whether or not you would abide by that value when making a choice.

One of my core values is freedom. I love my physical and locational freedom. I love that no one tells me when and where I have to be each day. I love that if I feel inspired to work at my office one day, I can go there, but if I feel like the vibe is going to be better at a coffee shop, I don't have to run that by anyone. I adore my freedom. Sounds pretty convincing, I know, but to test the value out, I had to think really deeply about whether it was important enough to inform my decisions.

For instance, if Google (which, btw, I worship) called me tomorrow, said they wanted to buy my company for twice its worth (humina, humina, humina), employ me at a comfortable salary (yay, stability!), let me live in San Francisco (dream city), and give me great, intelligent coworkers (bank), but I had to be at the office in the same seat at nine every morning and I couldn't leave that place until six that night, would I turn that opportunity down? For me, the answer is a resounding *hells yes!* I wouldn't even consider that role, because I know how important my freedom is to me. By doing this exercise, I have circumvented the days, weeks, or even months of agonizing about this decision when Google finally does call. I will know (almost without thinking!) that this job is not for me. That's how solid your core values can be. So test them out to make sure that each one of them is strong enough to withstand even the most enticing opportunities that aren't right for you.

Also, importantly, you'll want to test these values against each other and put them in order. Ask yourself if freedom or integrity is more important to you. This will be tough because they're *both* important. But force yourself to arrange your values in order, so that you have a waterfall of values that you can test your decisions against in the future. When you're done with your core values, you will have a record of everything that's important to you, prioritized, and written in language that deeply resonates with you. All that's left to do is pop a bottle of champagne to celebrate. Oh, and one more thing . . . turning these core values into commitments.

"Freedom is not the absence of commitments, but the ability to choose—and commit myself to—what is best for me."

PAULO COELHO

YOUR CORE VALUES
ON STEROIDS

REMEMBER THAT EXECUTIVE speaker with the spread-sheets from the previous chapter? He taught me another lesson about core values: they mean nothing unless you live by them. You must turn your values into *commitments*. You may have charity written down as a core value, but if you don't *practice* charity by giving of your time, talents, or treasures, is it truly a core value? You may deeply believe in integrity, but if you don't *practice* it by always aligning your words with your actions, is it truly a core value? The reason core values get a bad rap (especially in companies) is because most of us rarely make the leap from a nice list of words to a set of rules that dictate our actions. Commitments are your core values on steroids. Creating commitments from your core values brings them to life, shows you how to apply them in everyday situations, and helps you outline a clear vision for your future.

In addition to Mr. Spreadsheet (a.k.a. Russell Huber) writing out his morning routine in all of its self-affirming glory, he also shared with us a list of core values that he and his family live by. He believes commitments come first. With commitments, you can set goals, define habits that would move toward those goals, and ultimately have the best chance at achieving those goals. With values-driven commitments, you'll always know the basic parameters for success as you define it *and* you'll have a clear list against which to test your decisions. Here's the list he shared, which is just as intricate and individualized as the morning routine:

Stability in my life
Live in Dallas
Display and live consistent faith in my life
Job where I can make money and is not dramatically impacted by economic downturn
Mrs. Huber to stay home
Teach the kids to save
Live in old house
Eagle Scouts and Girl Scout Gold Award
Catholic schools and pay for public college
Live a long life and work until at least sixty-five[2]

At first, I thought, "Aww, that's nice. What a cute list of life goals. I tried that once! Too bad life had other plans…" What I didn't realize was how *serious* he was about these values, and how having these commitments—defined *ahead* of any decisions—equipped him and his family to make fast and powerful choices. For example, earlier that year, he had been contacted by a headhunter about a different senior executive position. The salary was higher. The benefits were better. The role was significantly more prestigious. All the shiny bells and whistles said this was the next logical step in his career. It would be crazy *not* to take it. The catch? The job was in Seattle.

Now, be honest. Even if you had committed to living in Dallas and had good reason to hold fast to that commitment, would you still consider making the move in this scenario?

If you're not an immediate "yes," I know for a fact that most of us would agonize for days or weeks about something like this. I mean, salary, benefits, status... Hello! This fruit is ripe for the picking! But what did *he* do? He doubled down on his values-driven commitment. He *didn't even blink* before saying, "Thanks, but no thanks. That doesn't hold with my family's commitments." He knew *immediately*, without stress, anxiety, or questioning, that this opportunity—while impressive—didn't align with his family's first two core values. He didn't allow himself to get caught up in the distracting details. He also put aside any emotion he felt about the opportunity *in the moment* and looked at the job objectively. By sticking to his commitments, he was living his values and he knew that those commitments would ultimately bring him and his family happiness. Incredible.

How to Make Commitments That Work

You too can perform such inspired feats of decision-making by transforming your core values from pretty words into actionable, tangible, and immediate commitments. We will get into the step-by-step process for doing so in the Become Unstoppable section at the end of this chapter. Here, I want to be ultra-clear about the difference between a value and a commitment. A core value encapsulates an idea, emotion, or virtue that you hold dear. Generally speaking, values describe or embody an *idea* rather than a metric by which you live. For instance, if love is a core value, that value itself doesn't necessarily dictate how you go out into the world and prove to yourself and others that love is important to you.

This difference between ideas and actions is why it's crucial to turn your values into commitments. Continuing with the example of love as a core value, there are many ways to define how to live it consistently. Perhaps you would commit to treating your romantic partner with respect or having at least one meaningful conversation with them per day. This type of tangible and actionable commitment not only makes your decisions easier but it also gives you a metric by which you can judge your relative success. I like to make daily, weekly, monthly, or yearly commitments related to my values. Here's an example using one of my values, "fully alive," which for me means feeling excited, eager, adventurous, and awake:

> **Daily commitment:** I do a meditation on joy during my morning gratitude practice.

> **Weekly commitment:** I reserve one evening/day per week specifically for play (coed softball, pub trivia, board games, and so on).

> **Monthly commitment:** I go on at least one out-of-town trip or other travel experience per month.

> **Annual commitment:** I create opportunities or participate in activities that give me a sense of adventure and excitement so I can feel eager about my life. (This is more of an ethos by which I live and/or make decisions.)

A PSA on Decision-Making

Every single person I've worked with has struggled to make sound, strong, decisive choices in their careers. No matter the situation, fear, doubt, or questioning arises in these scenarios. If you've every struggled to pick a restaurant, then you know what I'm talking about. Here's my humble theory about why this decision anxiety exists: our world has never before been more connected. We have more choices now, especially in our careers, than at any other time in human history. If you want to be a paid underwater basket weaver, you can find a way to do that. There's a guy who lives in Tahiti and makes a great living writing a blog about tree frogs, for crying out loud!

Not really. But did you even question it? I prove my point.

People all over the world are making a living doing things you would never imagine someone would pay for. It's happening. All the time! However, because of that luxury, we're left with a psychological dilemma of indecision. I call it the Peanut Butter Problem. Allow me to explain.

Imagine for a moment that you're a seventeen-year-old boy. Your mom tells you she needs to run to the grocery store for a few items the family needs. Naturally, you volunteer to run this errand out of the goodness of your heart (a.k.a. you want to drive with your newly minted license). She asks if you will get everything on the list, exactly as it says. Having gone to the store with her since you can remember driving that cart shaped like a Tonka truck (although admittedly never alone), you find this to be a ridiculous question. Of course you'll get *everything* on the list *exactly* as it says. How hard can it be? Before she can say another word, you snatch the keys and the list from her hand and sprint out the door and into the car. Windows down. Spotify on. Life. Is. Good.

You arrive at the grocery store feeling like the badass you know you are. "Pssshhht, grocery shopping. Why was she so worried? I got this," you think, as you scan the list's handful of everyday items. Seems simple enough, so peanut butter is where your grocery adventure begins. And that's when it happens. You round the corner, turn down the aisle, and ... your stomach falls out of your butt. There must be about 1,000 different kinds, brands, shapes, sizes, choices, and consistencies of peanut butter. *Peanut butter!* How, on God's green Earth, are you ever going to choose?

You check the list. It still just says "peanut butter." Nothing to clarify or qualify *which* peanut butter is the right one. You look back up at the wall of choices in front of you and begin to question your sanity. You try to think. "Well, there was that one time Mom got the creamy generic stuff, but Sarah didn't like the taste. But that's the least expensive. Maybe that's the one Mom wants. But she said something about our diets and used the word 'organic' over and over again. Maybe that's it. But that organic stuff has the weird syrupy-looking water on the top of it. That can't be right. And it's expensive. But it says 'healthy.' And what about sun-butter? Is it the same thing or different? Good grief, how am I ever going to figure this out?" It's enough to drive any seventeen-year-old boy to his knees.

Now, I know this is a bit overly dramatic, but compare this scenario to the last time you looked at a job board. Scrolling infinitely and trying to test the merits of one job against another. Did it feel akin to the kid staring at the wall of peanut butter? Did you feel overwhelmed by the sheer volume of choices while simultaneously underwhelmed by every single job? Did you not want to call Mommy? Everyone I've spoken to who lacks career clarity feels this way. And for most job seekers, choice overwhelm feels like an insurmountable problem. But thankfully, the cause of this conundrum is startlingly rational, which makes its solution fairly simple.

Beating the Peanut Butter Problem

A seventeen-year-old might stand paralyzed in front of a wall of peanut butter choices. A thirty-year-old job seeker might find herself rocking back and forth in a ball on the floor after thirty minutes on a job board. Both scenarios are created by the same problem: they both lack *clarity*. Think about it. If that grocery list said "all-natural, organic, no salt added, raw peanut butter," then the choices would dwindle from an overwhelming wall of peanut butters to just a few jars. Decision made. On your way.

This quality—clarity—is *exactly* what you need in your career search. Clarity leads to specificity. A lack of clarity leads to generality. The last time you went to a job board or had coffee with a friend or called your parents out of career desperation, what were you looking for? A *job*? *Something* you love? A bigger *paycheck*? What do all those desires have in common? They lack precision. They aren't clear. They don't pinpoint any one pursuit in particular. As a direct result, your search isn't gaining any traction.

No matter how honorable your intentions, your lack of clarity and specificity will always leave your search process wanting. You could have the desire to change the world, but until you know how, for whom, with what, and when (just to name a few details!), you're going to be left confused and bewildered like a seventeen-year-old in the peanut butter aisle. However, if you have even a handful of specific, clear, tangible *commitments* around the type of peanut butter career you want, then you'll quickly see which options are viable and which are not. Your number of choices will dwindle just like the jars in my example. You'll be on the fast track to making career decisions as though you had an Easy Button at your side.

In addition to limiting your choices to a digestible amount, a clear set of commitments will help when you are choosing between one course of action or another. For example, if one of your core values is family and your resulting commitment is living within driving distance to your parents, then you can easily narrow down your job search to a specific geographical location. That's a simple example and may sound so straight-forward that it's worth skipping. However, it's a real-world solution to the real-world problem of where to live or even where to begin your job search. If you have a core value of stability, for instance, and the resulting commitment of having a steady nine-to-five, it's probably best not to entertain ideas of founding a business or working in a start-up. Those options would be what we in the biz call non-starters. This level of specificity narrows your choices and equips you to make stronger decisions.

Creating Crystal Clear Commitments

Ever heard the phrase "When you speak to everyone, you speak to no one"? This quote, often attributed to Meredith Hill, speaks to a widely held belief in the marketing world. If your messaging is written to appeal to everyone, it won't deeply reach anyone because it lacks specificity. In other words, when you try to make everyone happy, you give up your laser focus. Generalities lead to watered-down, weakly articulated messaging that fails to reach the specific person you want to serve. If that person can't see themselves in your advertising, they move on to the next shiny option. Why does that matter for you? Because the same is true for your career search.

If you're not focused in your job search, you become a human version of watered-down advertising. First of all, it makes you confusing. Second, your "messaging" won't have the impact you need because it won't land with anyone in particular. There's a serious difference between a job seeker saying "I'm keeping my options open" or "I'm looking for

Your commitments
are **your core values
turned into actions.**

anything," and someone who says "I was made for this" or "There's no one better at this than me." That laser focus is the difference between a job search based in vaguely defined parameters and one based on *commitments*. It's logical to think that the first person will have more opportunities than the second, but that's not how it works in the real world. While one person looks like a generic employee, the other person is selling themselves as a unique asset. Which person do you think companies want to hire?

The trick here is creating clear commitments. Vague commitments won't cut it. Your role in the career search process is to create as clear a picture as possible of your ultimate pursuit. It's your duty to devise your core commitments not only because they will make your decisions easier but also because they put you directly on track for achieving your goals and reaching your *ideal* career. Commitments will become the basis for your decisions and basic parameters for your life as you move forward. In my experience, working from your core values is the best and most straightforward way to make commitments. In fact, if your core values don't inspire some type of commitment on your part, then they probably aren't core values. To turn your core values into core commitments, ask yourself these three important questions:

1 Why is this value so important to me?
2 What happens if I don't have this core value?
3 What will I commit to that proves to myself and the world that this core value really matters to me?

The answers to these questions will be different for everyone, even if the core value is similar. Two people could have a core value of playfulness, for instance. One might commit to sixty minutes of child-like play per day, and the other might commit to being a kindergarten teacher to stay close to the joys of childhood. I have no idea how you will answer these three probing questions. I do know that by answering them, you will start to create core commitments that will allow you to weather the storms of decision-making without being driven by in-the-moment emotions. You'll know that no matter what sparkly, fun, or outrageously cool-sounding jobs come your way, you have a foolproof method for making the right decision for yourself. The structure will set you free!

A quick note for the cynics: you may have a negative reaction to making commitments, feeling that they're limiting. Creating a set of non-negotiable core values and commitments may feel restrictive, but that's the point. Commitments are meant to be limiting so that you stop entertaining horrible jobs and non-starter careers! Commitments allow you to dodge the options that you would never really like anyway! Embracing this process narrows down your search to include only the opportunities that align with who you are and what you want to do. It eliminates fruitless distractions. Trust me. This works.

BECOME UNSTOPPABLE: YOUR CORE COMMITMENTS

Step 1: Gather your list of core values.

Make sure your values are already:

1 narrowed down to approximately ten,
2 true for you, and
3 listed in order of importance.

Step 2: Ask yourself the three clarifying questions about each core value.

1 Why is this value so important to me?
2 What happens if I don't have this core value?
3 What will I commit to that proves to myself and the world that this core value really matters to me?

Step 3: Create your first set of core commitments.

This is much simpler than it sounds. Based on the answers to the questions in step 2, write a statement that will serve as a rule or requirement for how you live this value. Think about a daily, weekly, monthly, or annual commitment. Consider how each core value lends itself to a way of life.

For example, a recent client's number-one core value was "a Midwestern way of life." To him, that meant more ease and less stress. This was important to him because he felt more joy when he was in a laid-back environment. When he was living in Dallas, he felt like life was zooming by and he could never relax or enjoy anything. So, how did he translate that value? His commitment was to move to Kansas City, live closer to his family, only pursue work within a certain area, and leave Dallas as quickly as possible.

These parameters allowed him to easily say yes or no to any job opportunity. He knew, without agonizing or questioning himself, whether a job was viable or not. His commitments also narrowed down the list of viable businesses and roles he wanted to pursue. All in all, defining that value and making commitments around it led him out of Dallas in less than a month, and he was working in the job of his dreams in less than six!

**Step 4: Write down your commitments and
share them with at least two people.**

Your commitments aren't real unless you act on them, so share
them with two people you trust, and start practicing account-
ability to your commitments each and every day. As a litmus
test, envision what type of yes-or-no decisions you would
make based on each of your commitments. If a commitment
doesn't clearly dictate an aspect of what is within your set of
acceptable actions, behaviors, or metrics, then it's too vague.
Refine it until you have a list of commitments that really mean
something to you and help you envision making faster, easier
decisions.

"In order to carry a positive action
we must develop here a positive vision."

DALAI LAMA

5

CREATE A CLEAR
CAREER VISION

WHERE DO YOU see yourself in a year? Three years? Five years? Ten years? Does that question freak you out or motivate you to pursue your vision? Chances are, if you've had a less-than-ideal career for any particular amount of time, these are among some of the hardest questions to answer. When we're not happy with our circumstances and we can't access a sense of possibility, it's hard to create a vision for the future. That's why, at this phase, it's essential to connect your life audit, core values, and commitments and use them to identify a clear *vision* for your ideal future. If you can see it, you can achieve it. But first you need to see it.

Why Your Vision Is So Powerful

I'm not saying you need to have an actual, physical vision board onto which you post phrases or pictures (but they are pretty fun and handy). What you *definitely* need is a tangible vision—written or typed—that calls to you along your path.

Without a clear vision, you lack focus. Think again about the "speaking to everyone or no one" idea from the exercise on commitments. When you lack clarity of vision, your attention—a finite resource—is split up. You become drawn to distractions that have no connection to your ideal future state. Sure, you might still reach your goals, but instead of your path being as efficient as possible, it will be long, winding, and confusing. When your attention is divided instead of focused on a unified and specific goal, your motivation dissipates. That means when the going gets tough, you might take the easy way out.

I know this to be true, because it happened to me about a year before I started my own business. After Semester at Sea, I knew three things for certain. I needed a remote or flexible job so that I could continue to explore my options. I wanted to work in the industry of talent and development. I hoped to deliver significant value to people's lives. Those were my very first conscious commitments. To that end, I began working remotely for a woman who trained organizational leaders in empathy, diversity, and inclusion. Check, check, and check! Yahtzee!

For a while, everything was fine. I was living in line with all of my commitments and proactively pursuing my ideal career. Then, as they say, life started to happen. My income wasn't high enough to be sustainable, so I started working side jobs in retail and restaurants. My boss decided that she wanted to close her business and return to a corporate setting, so I was about to be out of a full-time job. All of a sudden, fear and doubt and anxiety set in. I got scared that I would not find anything, and I allowed that limiting belief and fear to take over—outweighing my core values, commitments, and vision. As a result, I took the first full-time job that came my way without doing anything that resembled due diligence. I was required to be in the office from nine to five (not remote), working on client success for corporate entities (not talent and development), and I spent my days focused on typos and misplaced pictures in software systems (not significant). And you know what happened?

I. Got. Fired.

I got fired! Not only that, but I had been miserable in that job from day one, biding my time and hoping that nobody would notice. I had lost sight of my vision. I had taken a job that was a terrible fit for me out of fear. And I had to suffer through the most humbling experience in my adult life, because my vision, focus, attention, and motivation had disappeared.

I tell you this story because I hope it serves as the only cautionary tale you need. Don't make this mistake yourself. Quitting your job might be scary. Taking a professional risk to find your ideal career may be daunting. But getting fired from a job that you didn't even like in the first place? Trust me—that feeling is worse.

Thankfully, I learned from that ~~mistake~~ lesson. Now, I work hard to maintain and pursue a clear vision for my business. Even when I go through hard times (which I promise are many), I remind myself of my vision for the company, the impact we can and will have, and the lives that we are changing. I keep that vision in mind so that I can maintain focus on what matters. I channel my attention to those tasks only, which bolsters my motivation and my productivity. Am I always perfect at this? No. It's a continuous practice, like anything else. But just because you won't have mastery right away does not mean this strategy isn't worth pursuing.

If You Build It, They Will Come

The law of attraction, which was popularized in *The Secret* by Rhonda Byrne, is the idea that the more we focus on something, the more we get of it.[3] The law rests on the belief that

Think about your goal, envision your end state, **and then figure out everything you need to do to get there.**

all our interior thoughts eventually manifest in the exterior world (what we believe, we become). The more we concentrate on something in our minds, the more we attract of it into our physical lives.

This idea may sound kooky, but you know it to be true. Think about that friend who's a Negative Nancy. Don't bad things always seem to happen to her? Or what about Positive Polly? Doesn't she always seem to get free stuff or have really cool, unexpected experiences? Nancy is not negative because bad things happen to her, and Polly is not positive because good things happen to her. It's the exact opposite. Their mindsets *create* their perception which in turn encourages the different realities they live in. Whether you believe or acknowledge this idea, you are constantly attracting a certain type of reality and energy to yourself. In short, you're co-creating your everyday experience.

Thankfully, we can use this phenomenon to our advantage. If you consciously create a vision for your career—you think through that vision and use words or pictures to define it—you harness the law of attraction and use it for your own benefit. You don't even have to be a way-out-there hippie to believe this. Cognitive science backs up this law in that our brains are hardwired to see the things we think about the most. Recall the earlier example of the newly purchased car that suddenly turns up everywhere you look. The brain forces us to see, focus on, and attune to whatever we spend our time thinking about the most. Why not use this to your advantage? Think about the ideal role, career, and lifestyle that you want at this phase of your life. You won't be handed everything on a silver platter just because you "thought it into being," but you will notice opportunities you didn't see before you were focused on your vision—introductions will be made, dots will be connected, possibilities will arise—and all of this will seem coincidental, but in reality, you'll be creating it for yourself.

One of my favorite sayings from my years in athletics was "act like you've already been there." If you're in the championship game, and you're experiencing doubt and anxiety because you've never played at such a high level, the best thing you can do is to act like you've been there to counteract that fear. You can use this mantra in professional situations too. If your dream is to become a photographer, start referring to yourself as a photographer. Even if you're just starting to take classes and setting up your commercial website, you are, in fact, a photographer. So, why not embrace it and act like you've been there? If your dream is to become a data scientist, then refer to yourself as a data scientist while you're taking classes at night. Your mind is powerful, so use it to your advantage.

Using Your Audit to Create Your Vision

The easiest way to keep the vision-creation process simple is to do a life audit in reverse: look at the same eight major areas of your life that we explored in your audit (emotional, environmental, financial, intellectual, physical, professional, social, spiritual), think about your ideal state, and use them as a framework to define your vision for the future.

What comes to mind when you imagine each facet in its ideal state? Skip nice-to-haves or yeah-maybes or sure-that-sounds-goods. Go for *ideal*. One of my business coaches always says, "The energy with which you create will be inherent in your creation," so a small piece of advice here. While you're envisioning your future: smile! While you're imagining your ideal state, get excited. There should be a lot of smiling, fist-pumping, and "hells yes!"-ing going on during this process. If not, you're aiming too low. Don't hold back. Place the vision for your ideal future squarely in your mind and begin to put it out into the world through words and images. Don't be surprised if some very interesting opportunities come your way.

BECOME UNSTOPPABLE:
YOUR REVERSE LIFE AUDIT

Step 1: Write down the eight major categories of your life.

In a notebook or a digital document, write down each of the eight categories (emotional, environmental, financial, intellectual, physical, professional, social, spiritual) at the top of its own page.

Step 2: Review your previous life audit for insight.

Remember how you segmented your life audit into what was going well and what could improve? Use those notes as inspiration in this exercise.

Step 3: Ideate your ideal future state.

Set a timer for five minutes. During that five minutes, jot down what immediately comes to mind when you think about the ideal manifestation of each category; repeat for each category. Ready to get married? Write it down. Want to be a titan of industry? Write it down. Want to travel four times per year? Write it down. Remember we're going for ideal *right now*, so keep in mind your current unchangeable circumstances. Look for intersections of your responsibilities and your values and commitments to find the ideal future state that is realistic *and* attainable.

"The most difficult thing
in life is to know yourself."

THALES OF MILETUS

6

EFFECTIVELY TURN
THE LENS INWARD

AT YALE, I studied psychology. It only took one class, Intro to Psych, to figure out that I loved to learn about people. Behaviors, motivations, emotions, attractions, relationships, you name it! I was hooked. And because Yale's curriculum was so research heavy, it seemed like we were discovering new universal truths about human psychology nearly every week. However, no matter the number of discoveries we made, there was always one unanswerable question: are we as human beings more defined by our nature or are we more of a product of how we're nurtured? In fact, Yale had an entire class devoted to this question aptly titled Nature versus Nurture. I elected not to take the class, because I could surmise the answer from the start.

We're a product of both.

In the following chapters, you're going to be exploring what makes you *you*. Specifically, we're going to look at both your Nature and your Nurture: how is your professional value dictated by your inherent nature (behaviors, gifts, aptitudes) and how is your professional value shaped by your experiential nurture (skills, knowledge, expertise)? I like to think of these two components as opposite sides of the same coin.

In this process, Nature encompasses all of your traits—behaviors, preferences, and talents—that come to you naturally. These traits make up what we might call your gifts and your personality. The amazing thing about your nature is that some of it (like your core behavioral preferences) is solidified at a very young age, while other parts (like your strengths) are revealed over time. You set yourself up for success if you properly leverage your nature by pairing your natural tendencies with your salient work environment—a.k.a. bringing your whole self to work.

Exercises within Nature explore how you show up when you're simply being yourself both in personality and behavior and then what talents or gifts you can leverage to succeed with less effort.

Nurture encompasses slightly different but just as important traits—knowledge and skills—that you've gained over time. These traits arise from your experiences and make up what we might call your expertise or collective genius. Our nurture is always growing and changing. We can add to it, both purposefully and accidentally, at any time. You properly leverage your nurture when you take advantage of all your education, work, and seemingly unrelated life experiences to add the maximum possible value, without wasting anything in the process. Exercises within Nurture illuminate the various and cumulative experiences you've had in life which have added knowledge, skills, and expertise to your professional toolkit and how you can maximize them for success in the future.

The goal here is to continue in our discovery of what makes you special and sets you apart from the career crowd. Together, we'll go deep into Nature and Nurture to mine them for gold—the nuggets of your true professional value based on the unique individual that you are. We're going to see what you can learn and leverage from each of these influences and how to relate them to your career.

A word of advice as you begin: stay in fact-finding mode. As you dig for information, try not to assume, infer, or conclude anything before the mining is complete. Resist putting any puzzle pieces together before you have the full set. Avoid the temptation to jump to the end and embrace the steps in the process instead. The Nth Degree methodology has worked for everyone who's diligently completed these steps before you, so you can trust in the process. It works.

So, let's begin with the first exercise in discovering your Nature.

Are You a Cow or a Dolphin?

I have a fun little thought experiment that proves the real impact and importance of knowing your nature. Imagine, for a moment, that you're a cow. (I promise I'm going somewhere with this.) You're a cow in a field surrounded by hundreds of other cows. You're eating grass. You can see for miles into the grassy distance. The sun is shining bright, puffy clouds are slowly passing by. All you can see are rolling hills, grass, and other cows. Ah, life is good. You are one happy cow.

Now imagine that you're a cow... suddenly dropped in the ocean. You try to swim, but you've never even been in the water before. You try to eat fish, but you've only ever eaten grass. You try to speak dolphin, but you've never even *seen* a dolphin before. And no matter how hard you try, those dolphins are swimming circles around you and laughing, you know, as dolphins do.

If someone tries to tell you that nature doesn't matter—that you can be just as successful anywhere if you "put your mind to it" or "keep working hard"—remember what it mentally felt like to be a cow in the ocean. Maybe some of you have had this kind of experience professionally. I know, in my first role, that felt out of place constantly. I told myself that this was part of the learning curve and would get better. In the process, I fought my nature. I convinced myself that if that job equaled success, then I was a failure for not making it work. For some reason (probably because human beings are more similar to each other than cows are similar to dolphins), we assume we can all function in any environment if we work hard enough. Unfortunately, when it comes to our careers, this is simply not the case. Yes, if you work hard, you have a better chance of succeeding. But if you identify an environment that suits you like a grassy field does a cow, you have a much better and easier chance at success.

What Happens When We Deny Our Nature

You were created for something unique, something special. There is, right now, a career out there that will fit you like a hand in a glove, but only if you're open to exploring and accepting your true nature. Doing so is hard, because we don't live in a world of cows and dolphins. We live in a world with Rob in accounting, Susan in marketing, and Marie in sales. It might not be glaringly obvious that any given job isn't your proverbial ocean or field, so living this reality requires deep self-knowledge and self-acceptance.

Take one of my best friends, Julie, for example. Julie inadvertently became one of my first clients when she seemed especially tired one day. I asked her what was going on, and she said that work was exhausting her. At that time, she was employed at a specialty doctors' office. In the same way that pharmaceutical reps visit various doctors to sell prescription drugs, she visited the offices of general practitioners to persuade them to recommend their patients to her group of specialists. Although some of us would love bringing break-fast, lunch, and snacks to doctor's offices and shooting the breeze with physicians all day, it made Julie miserable.

My business was in its early days, but I had already started using a particular behavioral assessment for clients and within companies. I figured that giving the assessment to Jules couldn't hurt, and so she spent five minutes completing it, in the hopes that we'd discover something to help make her days easier. We found that Julie wasn't just working in a challenging environment, she was completely ignoring her nature. In fact, she was forcing herself to be somebody else—like a cow competing with dolphins in the ocean—for eight hours a day.

The assessment suggested she was the type of person who didn't like to rock the boat (not so suitable for sales). She functioned best in small groups or in one-on-one interactions with very little conflict. She loved being of service and seeing the fruits of her labor. But what was she doing all day? Schmoozing doctors. Driving around alone for hours. Praying the doctors would refer patients, without having a way to measure her success. Persuading people. Not only had she turned herself inside out, but her inherent and natural *strengths* had almost become *liabilities*. She was a glorious, one-of-a-kind, talented "cow," but she was flailing out in the ocean, trying to compete as a dolphin.

What Makes You Unique

Human beings tend to have natural preferences—good and bad—for particular ways of thinking, feeling, and acting. To separate what is innate from what is learned, scientists have examined humans who are genetically identical but have

Imagine being completely yourself, all day long, and being successful doing that.

different life experiences: twins. The results have shown that identical twins tend to correlate on a large number of traits—disease, behaviors, intelligence, and even divorce.[4] The heritability of certain traits suggests that at least part of who you are comes from genetics. Even twins separated at birth share similar behavioral profiles. This suggests that while your environment shapes you and teaches you many new strategies, the likelihood of your inner nature or personality changing is very low.

If that's the case (and science tells us it is), I say we stop trying to fight it. Let's embrace it and use it to our advantage, especially when it comes to our careers! Your unique innate behaviors, thoughts, and feelings represent your natural *genius zone*. These are the activities that you do well, without even having to think about them or expend lots of effort. By aligning those components of your nature with your salient career environment (think dolphin in the ocean), you give yourself a leg up on the competition. This alignment is the best chance of succeeding on the path of least resistance.

At the end of the day, our contribution relies on our energy. You can either choose to spend your finite amount of energy in one of two ways: working on the task at hand or modifying who you are and then using the leftovers to do your work. By creating alignment between your nature and your career, you give yourself the best chance to succeed, simply by being yourself. You become the proverbial cow in the field or the dolphin in the ocean. In my professional observations and experiences, such alignment shows massive increases in effectiveness, efficiency, and job satisfaction. And who doesn't want that?

In the end, Julie switched career gears to align with her nature. Fast-forward to today, and she has a business as a nutrition advisor, and she could not be happier. She has the freedom and flexibility she wants. She gets to serve others and has immediate, real-time feedback about her effectiveness. And she does this in a non-threatening, supportive, helpful environment that she creates for her clients. She cracked the nature code. And you can too.

How to Uncover Your Nature

I already know what you're thinking. "Tracy, if I *knew* what came naturally to me, I wouldn't be reading this book in the first place!" That's totally fair. In fact, oftentimes our natural and innate value is the most challenging attribute to identify about ourselves. As one of my business coaches aptly put it, "Doing introspection on yourself is like a talented cardiothoracic surgeon trying to do open-heart surgery on herself. Her perspective is off, the process is really messy, and the procedure is not likely to end well." Instead of fighting the reality that it's inherently challenging to be objective about ourselves, we have to try a different approach.

You don't have to go it alone. You don't even have to figure this out in your head or do some type of vast, deep introspection to uncover these traits. In fact, discovering your unique behaviors and personality is exactly what assessments were created to facilitate. When it comes to assessments, you've probably seen a few of them already. Our culture is particularly fond of tools like Myers-Briggs and DISC. My recommendation on assessments is this: the more the merrier! Because we're still in the Nature step, you'll want to look for assessments that measure relatively *fixed* assets. (We'll save our exploration of your flexible assets for the Nurture chapters to capture the assets you develop over time.) While we're exploring your Nature, we'll focus on natural gifts, talents,

By creating **alignment between your nature and your career,** you give yourself the best chance to succeed at the highest level.

behavioral drives, motivating needs, reactions under pressure, and the like. These are the qualities of who you are at your core—the most fundamental components of your nature.

When it comes to the wide world of assessments, I recommend these in particular and break them down for you below:

Predictive Index (behavioral assessment)
StrengthsFinder or HIGH5 (strengths assessments)
Myers-Briggs Type Indicator or 16 Personalities (personality assessments)
The RHETI (Enneagram "type assessment")

The Predictive Index (PI) measures who you are under pressure and stress, your core habits, and your most likely observable behaviors. I've seen this assessment give incredible insights across industry and age, because it specifically speaks to the ideal professional environment for each "pattern" it creates. I highly recommend using it, and I've used it professionally for years.

StrengthsFinder and the HIGH5 assessments gather information about your strengths: where and how you perform at your best. Better yet, they give you actionable, clear words like "activator" or "maximizer" or "connectedness" to help you articulate those strengths in detail. These assessments are relatively easy to find online. There is a small fee to use StrengthsFinder; the HIGH5 is free.

Myers-Briggs and 16 Personalities are among the most widely used personality tests. They break down our personalities into four competing pairs of traits that result in one of sixteen different personality types. If you hear someone say, "Oh yeah, I'm an ENFP," then they're talking about Myers-Briggs. I tend to use the 16 Personalities test, which uses exactly the same science and the website is unrivaled in providing easy, accessible information.

The Enneagram system of personality typing describes "types" defined by how you conceptualize the world and manage your emotions. Your results label you as one of nine numbers, each with its own subtypes, called wings. You can learn an incredible amount of information about yourself based on your core type and wings including behaviors, preferences, and pitfalls. The Riso-Hudson Enneagram Type Indicator (RHETI) test is even longer than its name, but the results are incredibly in-depth and almost limitless in their application.

All of these assessments offer certification for coaches, so if you find a coach or mentor, it's worth asking if they carry any of these credentials.

Here's the big takeaway: to get back to yourself, stop trying to do all the heavy lifting alone. Self-awareness is not always easy. In fact, a lack of it is probably why you've been dissatisfied with jobs in the past. However, if you commit to this—to learning more about yourself and being honest about who you really are—I can promise you won't be disappointed. You will discover your behavioral genius zone, and no one will be able to take that away from you. You'll know where you shine with the least amount of effort and the environment in which you can make your maximum impact and reach your fullest potential.

BECOME UNSTOPPABLE:
YOUR FIRST ASSESSMENTS

Step 1: Explore behavioral assessments online.

Check out the six assessments (Predictive Index, Strengths-Finder, HIGH5, Myers-Briggs, 16 Personalities, the RHETI). There are free and/or inexpensive ways to take all of them, and each one provides a significant amount of information online to take your results to the next level.

Step 2: Take many types of assessments.

Some of these tests can be done quickly (the PI takes five to seven minutes), while others take more time (the full RHETI has 144 questions). Some measure strengths, others personality, and still others motivations and drives. Each will give you a unique perspective on what makes you tick. Do them all in a relatively short period of time—within the same week, say—but release yourself from any pressure to do them all in one sitting, lest you get assessment overload. Take breaks.

Step 3: Explore your results.

These assessments provide interesting and intricate classifications and results, about which the body of knowledge is massive. Don't give in to the overwhelm, but do explore your results thoroughly. Specifically, you'll want to begin translating these results from generic to professional. Start to ask yourself some critical questions. Below is a by no means comprehensive list. Start here and allow yourself to brainstorm more applications as you go.

Where does this behavior show up in my current role?

Do any of these traits not get a chance to shine in my current role?

Does this result explain why I feel [insert emotion] about my job?

If I had a job that maximized this aspect of myself, would I be happier/more fulfilled/feel more purpose-filled/have more energy?

Step 4: Record your major insights.

Wherever you're storing your values and commitments, record your insights about your behavioral assessments. Resist the urge to make conclusions or assumptions about your career trajectory at this stage. Simply continue on your fact-finding mission and add your major insights about your nature to your existing insights from Now.

"Always keep an open mind and listen to what those around you have to say about you. You might actually learn something that may help you become a better person!"

AULIQ-ICE

7

SEE OTHERS AS
VALUABLE MIRRORS

I N THE WORLD of psychology, there's an iconic image of a kitten looking into a mirror and seeing a lion reflected back. The image is meant to remind us that what we believe about ourselves directly impacts how we perceive ourselves in the world. In this case, the perception can be an empowering and positive influence on our self-esteem and our self-image. However, if you're reading this book, you've probably had times (maybe even now) when the "mirror" (a.k.a. your self-concept) was your worst enemy rather than your best friend. You might be experiencing this phenomenon currently—in reality you have the heart of a lion, but in the mirror, you see a tiny, scared kitten.

Human beings create identities for ourselves all the time— for better or worse. We use these identities as shorthand to understand ourselves and how we fit into the external world. An influencer recently told me, "Your words become your world." For example, if you always think of yourself as bad at math, then over time that becomes part of your identity, and it is extremely difficult to overcome. In psychologist Carol Dweck's seminal book, *Mindset*, she calls this phenomenon a "fixed mindset." She cautions us on the limitations of a fixed mindset as it can negatively affect our performance over a lifetime.[5]

Unlike changing your style of clothes when fashion trends shift, changing your mindset or beliefs can be challenging. Even if your identity's equivalent of Hammer pants no longer serves you, letting them go can be hard—especially if it's a negative identity. The human brain is hardwired to guard against change, because it interprets change as potentially life-threatening danger. That also means your brain harbors negative thoughts ("you can't win at basketball") as a mechanism for safety ("so don't even try"), thus avoiding failure. This mechanism continues even though you know that it makes you feel miserable ("I suck at everything"). But we're wired to do it for safety! Thinking you're not worthy of love may make you feel crappy, but it sure as hell keeps you from getting your heart broken. See what I mean?

Embracing the Positive Opinions of Others

One of the best ways to change a lingering negative mindset is to start welcoming in the differing—and more positive— opinions of others. Earlier I said that putting too much stock into what other people think can be dangerous. This advice is definitely true when it comes to the limiting beliefs and expectations of others that impact you and your life negatively. The key here is distinguishing, asking for, and letting in *positive feedback* from people who care about you. Instead of staring at your reflection in the broken mirror (tiny kitten), this exercise will require you to see yourself through the positive mirror in others (lion).

One of my favorite books of all time is *If Life Is a Game, These Are the Rules* by Chérie Carter-Scott. In the book, the author defines ten rules for being human, which may sound cheesy but turns out to be incredibly deep. Rule number seven is "Others are only mirrors of you."[6] When I first read that, I thought this woman was a kook. "I mean, come on! People are so different! I can't possibly *only* be seeing myself in other people." But as I read on, everything made sense. According to Carter-Scott, when you judge other people, whether you love or hate them, your judgment reflects something you love or hate about *yourself*. In fact, the very *reason* that you love or hate that trait about that person is *because* it reminds you of yourself. By embracing this idea, you take responsibility for the patterns in your interactions with others and these reactions can be traced back to a trait in you that needs your care.

I was blown away. "You mean that all those times when I was a child and other kids told me I was bossy, it wasn't because they were being mean? All those times when my softball coaches criticized me for not being coachable enough, they weren't just being jerks? All those times I've judged other people, I've secretly been worried about something that might be true about myself?" Yes. Yes. And unfortunately, yes.

The good news is if others are mirrors of our truer selves, then perhaps we can use this reality when we struggle to see the best in ourselves. The unfortunate truth about feeling at your worst is how that feeling causes us to relate to other people. When you least feel like reaching out to people, that is usually the most crucial time to do so. That's the catch-22 of being in a dark night of the soul or simply feeling stuck. You need other people to jar you out of your rut, but you don't want them to see that you don't have everything figured out. I don't blame you. I felt the same way. After I got fired, I really needed a shoulder to cry on and someone to tell me I was still worth something. Instead, I ordered Whataburger and drove around Dallas aimlessly for two hours unable to even utter the f-word (fired) let alone share my state with someone else. It wasn't until I hit my mental and physical breaking point that I finally let it out. That's okay. That's normal.

Leveraging Your Biggest Fans

You have another choice. When you struggle to come up with anything positive on your own, doesn't it make reasonable sense to lean on the positive opinions of others? Authenticity and vulnerability have insanely awesome benefits. By allowing others to see how you really feel, you create the space for them to support you. The Interpersonal Mirror exercise in the Become Unstoppable section below is hands down everyone's favorite exercise. It's going to require you to reach out to people you know, like, and trust, and ask for their favorite attributes about you. Your job now is to figure out who to reach out to for help.

Entrepreneur, author, and motivational speaker Jim Rohn famously said that you are the average of the five people you spend the most time with. Think about that. Objectively, right now, who do you spend the most time with? Who in that group knows you better than you know yourself? And most importantly, are you willing to be humble enough to seek their counsel?

You are not meant to go this alone. I have to remind myself of that all the time. Sometimes, especially during tough times, your friends are going to know you better than you admit to knowing yourself. Embrace that and thank God for that, because otherwise you'd be down in that hole for a lot longer than necessary. Even if you don't feel great about yourself right now, you're on the right path. And you've already taken the hardest step: starting.

The action item in this chapter is my favorite exercise for achieving the interpersonal mirror effect. I ask my clients to do this exercise when they want to tap into the inspiring people around them to learn more about their own nature and their true higher identity. The goal of the exercise is to record the input of others and add it to your running definition of your nature that began in the previous section with assessments. By soliciting the input of others, you'll get a well-rounded view of your inner nature and you'll account for any gifts, talents, or personality traits that you're blind to or don't appreciate because they come so easy.

We are innately social beings. And because of this, people *want* to help you. Seriously! They do! You just have to be willing to be open with them about what you need. Tell them how they can help you. And then listen to their answers for insight.

BECOME UNSTOPPABLE:
YOUR INTERPERSONAL MIRROR

Step 1: Choose twenty-five people closest to you.

Friends, family, colleagues, associates—you name it! Although twenty-five people may sound like a lot, realize that only a certain portion will receive your message and a smaller portion than that will actually respond. Do your best to reach out to that number, or close to it, and you'll likely end up with somewhere between ten and fifteen responses in all. That's a good enough sample size to see trends or patterns in their responses.

Step 2: Text, email, or carrier pigeon this one question.

Ask "What are the three best things about me?" Keep this really simple, so you don't overly influence the answers. Tell your contact that you're working on something for your career, and you only need to know what three things they think are the best of who you are and what you have to offer. You'll get some one-word answers, some novels, and everything in between.

Step 3: Record answers in whatever format you choose.

Compile all of the answers you receive in a document or spreadsheet. Record complete answers and don't edit! First, revel in the love and affirmation provided by your people. This is a feel-good, uplifting, affirming exercise with long-term benefits. When I did it, I realized that even when I felt at my worst, other people could still see my best. Every single one of my clients feels this way as their responses come in, and I get consistent feedback that this is their favorite exercise throughout the entire program.

Step 4: Look for and note patterns.

Take stock of your total responses, and begin to look for similarities among them. Ninety-nine percent of the time, my clients identify three to five answers that come up the most frequently. Many find that no matter who they survey—friends, family, colleague, acquaintances—all of the responses are relatively similar or fall under the same general categories. This should be edifying, not alarming! Realize that this outcome means, regardless of how hard you may be pretending or flexing, the *real you* shines through. In this case, the best of the real you! Embrace this truth, and leverage it in your favor.

Step 5 : Consolidate your insights for Nature.

Record your insights from this mirror exercise with those from your assessments. What do you see? Look for alignment or through-lines from each assessment to each piece of feedback from your network. More than likely, you'll see similarities across your strengths, your personality, your behaviors, and your motivations. This collective insight can be said to encompass your professional nature—how you're going to show up in the world both under pressure and when you're simply being yourself. Take some time to think critically about the best version of you, and record major insights that run through all of your Nature exercises.

"The proper function of man is
to live, not to exist. I shall not
waste my days in trying to prolong
them. I shall use my time."

JACK LONDON

8

CULTIVATE A NOTHING
IS WASTED MINDSET

WHEN I FINALLY made the decision to leave my first job, there was one thought that kept weighing me down. I was finally accepting that my natural qualities were being underused and I was excited to find my own professional genius zone. However, I couldn't shake the notion that I had wasted two and a half years of my life pursuing a career that I no longer wanted to do. Today, I hear this same concern from every person who wants to make a career change. While they're excited to find work they love, they can't help but feel like they wasted time.

In the first five years of my business, I learned that this perspective is a choice. You can go through life thinking that if all of your actions don't line up and can't be tied with a pretty bow, then you've wasted time. Or you can commit to leveraging everything possible from your previous experiences. The "wasted time" style of thinking is wrought with anxiety about whether you're in the "right place" at any moment in your career. The "nothing is wasted" mindset alleviates this fear by acknowledging where you are now, learning from where you've been, and using those experiences to guide your future decisions. This mindset is crucial to the next step, Nurture, in the Nth Degree process.

You can do two things with previous experiences: use them or lose them. Using your experiences means both learning from what you've experienced and mining those experiences for valuable assets like knowledge, skills, and expertise. Losing your experiences means writing off your previous work, education, or life lessons as wasted simply because it doesn't obviously align with the future. It means throwing away the opportunity to learn something about yourself and the world that could fundamentally improve your career and your life and even set you up for success in the future. Don't lose it. *Use it.*

Adopting a nothing is wasted mindset means looking back at everything you've done—personal or professional, liked or disliked—and finding the activities, people, roles, responsibilities, knowledge, skills, and expertise that you can take with you as you move forward in your career. You may hate some of the previous jobs or environments you've been in, but the entire experience wasn't wasted time. You must identify what was gained and figure out how you can leverage these assets going forward. This mindset means seeing value in your previous experience while freeing yourself to pursue a different future state. Nothing is wasted unless you waste it.

Old Habits Die Hard

Once you've accepted this mindset—that nothing is ever wasted unless you waste it—then you have to change your actions to reflect it. The last thing you want to do is fall into old habits. Instead of just surviving where you are right now, start making conscious choices to live your life differently based on what you've learned.

My client Dominique was a perfect example of this. Dominque came to one of our three-day workshops convinced that success would be figuring out her future in the corporate world. She had been working for about seven years in different administrative and business management roles, and she wanted to create a path to progress at her company. On day two, at the halfway point of the workshop, I could tell something wasn't sitting right with Dominque. We had discovered that her core values centered on family and service. She was passionate about helping women feel more comfortable about their bodies. Her nature was an independent innovator, undaunted by failure, and with an innate ability to thrive under pressure. She was also a naturally gifted influencer with the ability to make you feel comfortable sharing and opening up about yourself within minutes of speaking to her. But none of these insights made her happy.

She just couldn't see how all of this would fit in the corporate space.

I sensed that she was holding on to an old idea of success, instead of embracing a nothing is wasted mindset. When all her Now and Nature work pointed to a career that hinged on freedom, creativity, and service, why was she was dead set on elevating her career in a corporate setting? Her response was exactly what I expected: "This is all I've ever done. Isn't the goal here to become a success in *the corporate world*?"

Old mindsets require constant challenging. In that moment, I had to remind Dominique that working in corporate does not necessarily equal success. Instead, the goal was to identify *her unique* professional value and define an environment that would put that to good use. In the five years I'd been in career advising, about 40 percent of my clients had pursued non-corporate professions—entrepreneurship, freelancing, travel writing, small business, and the like. As I spoke, her entire demeanor changed. Having been given *permission* to *pursue* anything and redefine success, Dominique finally opened up about a business that she had always dreamed of starting—a line of exercise leggings that were designed for plus-size women. She had designs. She had samples. She even had a company name! Best of all, her Now and Nature empowered the idea that she would thrive as an entrepreneur.

So what does this have to do with Nurture? Because she had spent seven years as a business administrator, she also had the skills of time management, organization, and finance. We identified via the Nurture exercises how she could leverage these learned abilities to augment her Nature. She felt empowered to move forward with her business idea because her unique combination of Nature and Nurture made her the perfect package to promote her idea.

Dominique is not a unique example. Every person I've had the honor of coaching has been holding on to something for fear of having wasted their time. Either that, or they've questioned their readiness for the next pursuit because their work history didn't fit it perfectly. We can overcome these two fears by embracing a nothing is wasted mindset. You can free yourself from the shackles of your previous professional life. Better yet, you can prove to yourself that you're ready for the next step in your career because you've been unknowingly preparing for it all along.

It may take some time and effort to adopt this new way of thinking. We've been raised in a world of résumés without holes and a clear path up the corporate ladder. But if you truly want to pursue a career that is *ideal*, rather than one that is simply convenient or linear, then the nothing is wasted mindset is the fastest way to get there.

Relearning from Your Education

A few years ago, I picked up a book that changed the trajectory of my life: Michael Ellsberg's *The Education of Millionaires*.

In it, Ellsberg suggests that much of what makes people successful in today's world has little to do with what we learn in school and much more to do with what he calls success skills—selling, marketing, finding mentors, and making your work meaningful. He explains, in great detail, how millionaires learn and practice these skills to accomplish above-average financial success and make a difference at the same time.[7] Having been a straight-A student and teacher's pet who graduated fourth in my high school class and attended an Ivy League school, I was pretty unnerved while reading his book. I mean, why the hell had I worked so hard for grades and degrees if everything I achieved meant nada when it came to success in life and career?

Much to my chagrin, I realized there was a ton of merit to his point about real-world success versus traditional education. However, I wanted to practice the nothing is wasted mindset when I looked back at my academic career. The idea isn't to discount all of the technical knowledge that you've gathered from traditional schooling. Instead, we want to supplement this traditional knowledge with real-world, practical know-how that can turn ideas into reality. So, as you begin the Nurture step of the Nth Degree, you're going to take this dual approach: dig into your formal education for topics and specialties you learned *and* explore your cumulative life experiences for the real-world value they hold.

Formal and Informal Learning Experiences

You'll begin with your formal education. It's crucial for you to do a thorough download of all the things you've learned. I like to start from preschool—yes, preschool—and go all the way through to your highest level of education. You never know when that random accounting class your mom forced you to take your senior year in college might come in handy... You also never know what old passions or interests you might uncover as you go back through your formal education. At this phase in the process, I highly encourage you to write down your favorite subjects, classes, and courses—even the ones you haven't thought of or used in a while—to get a true picture of the depth and breadth of your formal education.

Then you'll move on to less formal educational experiences. After I left finance, I traveled on a Semester at Sea. This experience allowed me the opportunity to do a little unlearning. My previous success in academic settings was built on spending hours on reading assignments and days perfecting papers and studying for tests. Being back at school, even though my grades didn't really matter, I fell back into my old overachiever, academic habits. Eventually, I was encouraged to pull my head of the books and assignments and realize where I was—on a once-in-a-lifetime trip around the world. That's when I learned that some of life's great lessons happen *outside* the classroom.

There was social learning; living, eating, getting sick, and having to spend all your time in very tight quarters for four months changes your view of interpersonal dynamics. There was experiential learning; nothing teaches teamwork like having to plan, practice, and present a synchronized swimming demonstration for Sea Olympics, not to mention traveling around Burma unsupervised. And then there was the hard-fought, self-deprecating personal learning that everyone experienced whether they wanted to or not. There's nothing quite like ten straight days at sea between Hawaii and Japan to get you thinking existentially.

Think back on your own life. Ask yourself, "What did I learn when I wasn't *formally* learning?" Look at the classrooms of your life. What lessons did you learn—about yourself, about others, about your career, about life in general—outside your formal education? What can you take with you and what do you want to leave behind? Gather all these life lessons, write them down, and add them to your list of formal education. In many cases, these lessons may be the "education of millionaires" you never knew you had.

A PSA about Lifelong Learning

Free learning is everywhere! Your education began the moment you opened your eyes for the first time and it will continue until your last day on Earth. Some of these lessons are obvious but others you have to dig deep to find. Even if you didn't expressly pay for these lessons, what you learned is valuable. Furthermore, if you don't have a certification or a degree, that doesn't mean you're not an expert in something. Even the people who describe themselves as a "jack of all trades but master of none" have become experts at seeing the big picture. You don't have to be a certified expert to know that something is true. If a free learning experience taught you something insanely valuable about your career or something incredibly insightful about your life, don't let it go to waste. Capture that little nugget and carry it with you as you move forward.

You're going to dig deep into your education and stretch that nothing-is-wasted-mindset muscle as you begin with this first exercise in the Nurture step. If you've ever tried to change an old habit or start a new routine, you know that it won't be easy at first. As with anything new, it's self-defeating to expect to be perfect at something without practicing. The following exercise on leveraging your education is a straightforward way to get more comfortable with the nothing is wasted mindset.

BECOME UNSTOPPABLE:
FORMAL, INFORMAL, AND FREE EDUCATION

Step 1: Write down all your formal education from birth to present.

Record which subjects, teachers, and lessons you liked the most and which you liked the least. Then dig even deeper for the why behind these reactions. What was it about that particular teacher that got you so excited to learn? What was it about that particular subject that fascinated you to no end? What was it about that one class you simply couldn't wrap your head around that was so confusing or inaccessible? The key here is to start thinking broadly about these specific experiences, and draw some conclusions about yourself to keep in mind going forward. My favorite question in this phase? What (if anything) from your formal education do you want to *learn more about* or *stretch toward*? If you can't help but want to learn more about a subject or continue to explore an idea, you've got something that has sustainability and longevity.

Step 2: Write down what you've learned outside the classroom.

Brainstorm the lessons that you have acquired outside formal educational settings. Take stock of these and ask yourself what (if anything) you want to take with you going forward. Again, you'll want to dig into the why behind these experiences. It's great to know that you were good at something, but why were you good at it? It's awesome to acknowledge you hated a particular experience, but why did you hate it? Look for overlapping or complementary insights as they relate to your more formal learning.

Step 3: Record all of your insights.
(Facts only, no assumptions!)

Consolidate your insights from formal and informal learning. Again, you're looking for both what you can bring with you from an asset perspective and any valuable lessons that will help you make strong decisions as you move forward. Your Nurture section is only just beginning! In the coming chapters, we'll explore both your work experiences and seemingly unrelated life experiences to get a fuller picture of your nurture-based assets and value.

"Study the past if you
would define the future."

CONFUCIUS

9

THE VALUE OF THAT JOB
YOU COULDN'T STAND

THE NEXT LOGICAL place to look for skills, knowledge, expertise, and lessons that you don't want to waste is— where else?—your work experience. Even if you have some professional PTSD from your previous role, this step is incredibly important! To do this properly, you have to adopt the mindset that *all* your previous work has value. Yes, all of it. You can learn *so much* from any work experience, even if you'll never step foot in that kind of position or environment again. That means you'll be exploring every experience including the jobs that made you miserable. At the very least, if you had a horrible experience, you've learned an oh-so-valuable lesson. Nothing is too small to be leveraged.

Making This Work for You (Pun Intended)

I can already hear the questions screaming at me through the pages. "What if I *really* hated my last job? What then? Will this really work for me?" First of all, I *feel* you. Not only have I asked that myself, but I've worked with plenty of clients who were running *from* something well before they ran *toward*

Which will you choose: Courageously finding value in a job you hated or fearfully avoiding that experience forever?

something else. I've met nurses, psychologists, sales associates, construction engineers, and project managers who have had traumatic work experiences. If anyone can understand and empathize with what you're going through, I can. There was a time when I was opposed to even *thinking* about the trading floor, let alone trying to pull value from it.

The key to this seemingly overwhelming and unappealing task is just like any other—the only way to eat an elephant is one bite at a time. To find the real value in your work experience (especially when it was primarily negative), it's best to break the experience down into something more digestible (yes, puns!). Break down the whole into its various parts and examine them one by one. You may look back at one job and because it's under the heading of "employment I hated," all aspects of it seem bad. If I had to categorize my time at the bank as one thing only, it definitely wouldn't fall under the titles of "useful" or "leverageable." Breaking down your previous roles into the who, what, or whens makes your task a little bit easier. Additionally, this process allows you to identify specifics that you can leverage in the future.

Mining Your Experiences for Value

Start with something simple, such as the environment of your most recent or current job. Work environment can include items like the size of the company, number of people, location of the office, positioning of the desks or cubicles, time spent working alone or in teams, access to the outdoors or natural light, proximity to a computer screen, and the like. You can get a lot of juicy information by narrowly focusing on environment. For instance, based on your experience:

Do you like working for big companies or small?
Do you like working in the city or in the country?
Do you like having a dedicated desk in an office or working remotely?
Do you need to spend time outdoors or moving your body?
Do you prefer to work in close proximity to others or in isolation?

Next, look at all the facets of your previous jobs one by one—the people, your role, the subject matter, the level of engagement, et cetera. To make this easy, begin by asking yourself the six Ws—who, what, when, where, why, and how—of your career history thus far. Go backward, job by job, and draw conclusions about how you felt about each of these aspects. What worked for you? What didn't? The answers to these questions will deeply inform your future decisions.

This mining exercise can be especially exciting (for me, anyway) when you're at your wit's end in your current position. When I hear clients say things like "I might die if I stay here any longer" or "this place is sucking away my soul," then I know we're cooking with grease. In an initial career assessment, a client named Patricia wrote that she felt like she was slowly dying. I knew this exercise might be a challenge for her as she transitioned from running away from a negative experience to running toward a positive one.

Patricia had been working as a stylist and curator for a subscription box company. Her remote role kept in her in isolation for eight hours a day. What little feedback she received from clients was always negative, and she had very little flexibility or freedom in her day. Despite looking completely negative on the surface, we were able to gather a couple of key positive characteristics from that experience. She loved having a creative outlet (styling) and that her

Seek to find value in the time you spent doing something you didn't necessarily love so nothing is wasted.

choices were positively influencing people's lives (her clients). She acknowledged that having community and collaboration (not being isolated) in her day was extremely important. She also needed more freedom in her hours (a flexible work schedule) to honor her commitment to her family. We used these takeaways to inform her decision to pursue a career as a coach—someone who lifts up others, collaborates actively, and can see the impact of her work—and she became my very first employee.

There's almost no end to this mining process, if you look hard enough. The objective of the exercise is to find value in the time you spent doing something you didn't necessarily love. If you have more positive previous work experiences, all the better. Either way, don't let the wasted-time monsters win! Don't let that voice in your head tell you everyone else is ahead of you and you're somehow behind. By strategically learning from your previous jobs, you can jumpstart your future career and feel back on track.

BECOME UNSTOPPABLE:
YOUR WORK HISTORY INVENTORY

Step 1: Make a list of every position you've held.

I find it easiest to begin where you are now and work backward. Include unpaid work, internships, freelancing, part-time and full-time jobs, even that random business you started when you were a kid or the time you spent babysitting.

Step 2: Record the who, what, when, where, why, and how of each role.

These should roughly equate to the people, the subject matter, the hours, the work environment, the role, and how you executed it. This step is all about facts, so just get the details out on paper.

Step 3: Take a deep (and objective) look at your cumulative experiences.

Ask yourself what value each experience offered you. Perhaps you gained some sort of expertise, a tiny bit of exposure you loved, or a knowledge set that can be leveraged elsewhere. Although I never want to see a trading floor again, I am definitely grateful for the ability to read a balance sheet and income statement, which came in handy when I started my own business. I could *never* have seen that coming! Dig deep. Figure out what valuable lessons you learned from each component of your previous work experience.

Step 4: Record your insights.

What will you take with you? What will you leave behind? What can you leverage and what can you use to guide better decisions in the future? Record these items in your Nurture notes.

"If you do what you love,
you'll never work a day in your life."

MARC ANTHONY

10

YOUR SECRET SKILL SET

YOUR EDUCATION AND work experience deliver valuable lessons about your ideal career. Work is work and education is what we did to lead to work. But this simple connect-the-dots path isn't how it works for everyone. Take my client Chandler, for example. When we started working together, he was twenty-five years old and had *never* had a job he enjoyed, so work was harder to mine. He had also chosen his college major to please his parents, so he didn't see much value in that investment either. After completing his education and work experience exercises, we were still at a loss. No spark. Nothing inspiring. Just a string of forced choices that had left him the worse for wear and worried that he would never find work he loved.

I'll be honest—I was nervous! Chandler was the first person who had been through the Nth Degree process who couldn't find even a handful of solid, redeeming qualities from any of his education or work experience. I wondered if he was being stubborn and holding out on me (I remember being twenty-five!). However, as I dug deeper, it became clear he was being honest with me and himself. He didn't have any educational or professional experiences he liked, and he felt hopeless searching for inspiration.

Thankfully, I had an ace in the hole. Chandler's less-than-inspiring work and education history was perfectly fine. It turns out that the true value he would bring to his next workplace would come from an entirely different set of skills. I call them "ninja skills."

What the Heck Are Ninja Skills?

Somewhere in between working and going to school, you have been living a life. You travel, spend time with friends, volunteer, exercise, play games, date, or decorate. Your activities outside the workplace and the classroom can tell you more than you think about yourself and your ideal career. These chosen activities reveal what I like to call your ninja skills: passions, gifts, talents, or interests that you do simply because you want to do them. If you're creative, you can *incorporate* the insights from these ninja skills into your career. The only reason we don't do this readily? At some point we separated paid work from activities like hobbies, traveling, or extracurriculars. However, for some people, these ninja skills provide the best information to guide ideal career decisions. This is exactly what happened for Chandler.

He approached this final exercise in the Nurture step almost as his last hope to discover anything about his past that he could leverage for a successful and fulfilling future. Despite this fatalistic attitude, this exercise is precisely when the magic happened. Chandler's true passions existed outside his education and work history. His hobbies (music and small-format construction projects), his extracurriculars (group projects after school and volunteering), and his travels (teaching abroad in Spain) provided the most inspiration and insight. These experiences highlighted his ultra-unique talents and interests, because they reflected true passions.

These insights ended up informing Chandler's decision to pursue a career that had more creativity, innovation, collaboration, and travel opportunity.

Chandler had never put any stock in these seemingly unrelated experiences. He had defined work experience as formal education or paid employment in a nine-to-five office. But it was the activities he loved and pursued in his free time that really illuminated his long-term and sustainable curiosities and interests. By recognizing that he came alive when he did each of these seemingly non-work-related activities, he committed to leveraging them professionally. He was able to define his niche, cultural design and engineering, by prioritizing these "extracurricular" activities.

Relating the Unrelated

In seeking out your ninja skills, I recommend you look to three areas of your life: extracurriculars, hobbies, and travel.

Extracurriculars

The term "extracurricular activities" may bring up memories of college applications and forced volunteer opportunities (hello, soup kitchen). Even if you were compelled to participate in an activity outside school, you can find value and learning in it. When examining your extracurriculars, consider the things that you chose to do and the things you were made to do:

Spent some less-than-ideal time in a retirement home as a teenager? *What did you learn?*
Participated in an art competition in middle school? *What did you learn?*
Got nominated to a particular program or society in college? *What did you learn?*

Find out who you are when you're out of your usual environment.

Don't limit yourself to work-like experiences. Really push yourself to think of all the things you did outside of school: sports, dance, music, games, reading, volunteering. Allow your experiences in extracurriculars to teach you something about your career interests. Remember: nothing is wasted.

Hobbies

To this day, I love color. But it took years of soul searching for me to *remember* that I used to love to color and draw. Boring college assignments and a numbers-driven job had left me, well, bland. But when I cajoled myself to dig deep into my past, I recalled that an entire wall of shelves in our house growing up was dedicated to art supplies. I remembered spending hours with my grandfather learning how to draw cartoons and with my dad making model cars.

Keep in mind what makes you happy... or even what *made* you happy way back when. Hobbies are what you do *just because* you want to. You don't (or didn't) have a clear directive or reason for creating or coloring or singing or dancing. You just do it. And childhood hobbies are the earliest signposts into your true delights and passions.

Did I end up being a graphic designer? Obviously not. But I did get to use my passion for color and creativity to create my own brand and website. I set aside time for creative activities within my own business. So, look back on your childhood and young adulthood and try to remember what you did just because it was fun. If you need to, call up family or friends to ask them. They will happily share with you all the things you used to do so often that it became annoying—like drawing on the walls!

Travel

Travel is one of your best teachers. It shows you a real and raw side of yourself, for better or worse. It also teaches you about the world beyond the one you grew up in. This exercise is about investigating your travel experiences for lessons you learned or skills you accumulated while away from home:

How do you handle the pressure and stress of being somewhere foreign?
What do you do when plans go wrong?
What about problems or setbacks?
Are you best traveling solo or can you hang with the whims of a group?
What happens when you're out of your comfort zone?

And all this can be massively influential on your future career. If you hated being abroad because you didn't have the comforts of your daily life, ask yourself why. Perhaps a more steady or predictable career is right for you. Alternatively, if you thrive on adventure and not knowing exactly where you're going, ask yourself why. Perhaps you need to chase something with a little more risk involved. Either way, let your travel experiences teach you. Don't assume that there is one right way or one right answer. Be limitless in your thinking. Own and love what traveling can teach you.

Light-Up Moments

In all of these areas—extracurriculars, hobbies, and travel— what you're looking for are light-up moments. These are times when you were completely immersed in an activity and time stood still. Maybe you felt joy so pure that you weren't sure if you were awake or dreaming.

Light-up moments signal deeper passions. They serve as figurative lighthouses on the ocean of life. They lead you in the right direction for you, even when you're not sure which way to go. Learn from your past and really dig deep. I promise that the discoveries you make will be both eye opening and life affirming.

BECOME UNSTOPPABLE: YOUR NINJA SKILLS

Step 1: List your extracurriculars, hobbies, and travel experiences.

In the Nurture section of your journal or working document, make three lists of all your relevant activities outside work and education. Include even those you were compelled to do. It's best to do this in categories (extracurriculars, then hobbies, then travel) or chronologically (all three types of experiences from birth until now), so you have some continuity in your brainstorming, and nothing gets missed or overlooked.

Step 2: Reflect on each experience to identify your ninja skills.

Write out any significant moments or insights from each item on each list and review them. Which brought you the most joy? Which are the most valuable to you? What, if any, light-up moments did you experience? From this analysis, determine which are most valuable to you now and those you can see informing your career decisions going forward.

Step 3: Think deeply about your most valuable experiences.

Identifying an experience as valuable is half the battle. Eventually, to really leverage these insights in your career, you'll have to help others understand your conclusions. Why is the extensive traveling you did after college valuable to your career? Why is the penchant for coloring and drawing you had as a child useful in your work? Why is your passion for welding in your spare time material to your job? The answers to these questions will help you articulate how you can make these experiences relevant to your career. Perception is everything, and your next steps start with *your* perceptions. Understand the why so you can eventually share it with others.

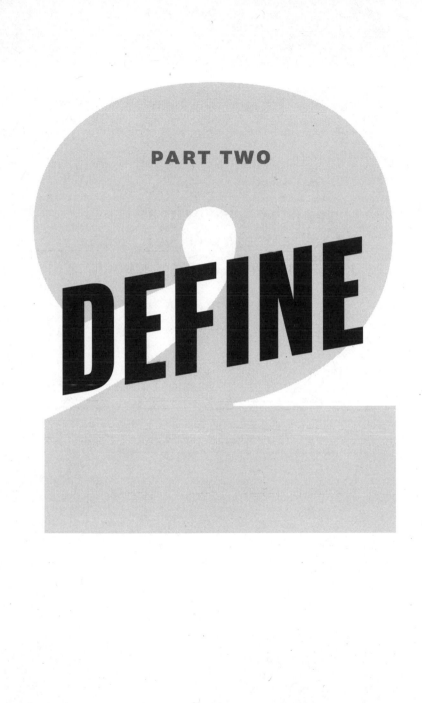

PART TWO

DEFINE

"Everybody is a genius. But if you judge a fish by its ability to climb a tree, it will live its whole life believing that it is stupid."

ALBERT EINSTEIN

ALIGNING YOUR PROFESSIONAL PUZZLE PIECES

ESPITE ITS CURRENT elusiveness, you probably know plenty of terms for a dream job:

Your sweet spot
Your sandbox
Your genius zone
Your fullest potential
Or, my favorite, your niche

The ideal career for you—your niche—is where you can add maximum value to your work and receive maximum value in return (salary being but one of many forms of value exchange). When you identify your ideal niche in the career marketplace, you'll no longer be "just" an employee—a *commodity* who's easily replaceable. Instead, you'll elevate yourself to the level of a unique, values-added, irreplaceable, and incomparable *asset*. You'll go from competing at the junior varsity level in someone else's event to winning Olympic gold in an event ideally suited for you.

Imagine three of the greatest Olympians ever. Let's use Usain Bolt, Michael Phelps, and Nadia Comăneci. These people are undeniably some of the best athletes who've competed in any sport—but they thrive in their respective events. Despite being amazing athletes, it would be unreasonable to expect each of them to achieve the same results in any *other* Olympic event. Begin to imagine careers like Olympic events. To ask you to perform at the highest level professionally in an "event" that doesn't suit you is a recipe for disaster and disappointment. To work in your niche requires you have a deep understanding of yourself and match that to your career. If you're Usain, leave the swimming pool and get on the track. If you're Michael, get off the balance beam and jump into the pool. If you're Nadia, exit the track and grab onto the uneven parallel bars. You can excel when you're perfectly matched to what you are uniquely suited to do.

Shifting the Career Search Paradigm

To begin, we have to shift your concept of the career search itself. Instead of trying to figure out where you fit in the professional world, we're going to do the process in reverse. You're going to create a vision of your ideal zone of genius— your niche—and then see what, in the professional world, fits you. This is a significant shift in how most people assume the career search works. When you elevate yourself from commodity to asset by becoming crystal clear on your professional zone of genius, you get back into the driver's seat of your own life. Instead of trying to figure out how your experience, education, and expertise align with a specific role, industry, or preexisting set of job requirements, you're going to do the opposite. Explore which companies, organizations, and work situations would be ideal for *you* based on your niche. Instead of companies or organizations interviewing you, in a very real way, you will experience the process the other way around.

To gain that confidence, you must master step 4 in the Nth Degree process: Niche.

How do you do this? I like to think of this part of the process as "career math." You're going to collect all the information you've gathered so far and explore how it all fits together. There's a simple framework in which you can leverage everything from the Discover phase and transition to Define to create your professional niche.

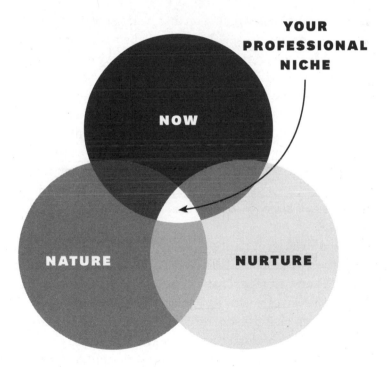

As you can see from the illustration above, you can conceptualize your professional niche as the nexus of your Now, Nature, and Nurture. I like to work with a Venn diagram in mind. When you identify a component of your Now (values, commitments, and vision) and where it overlaps with your Nature (personality and gifts) and Nurture (knowledge and skills), then you've identified one crucial component of your Niche. Repeat this process for all the components of your Now, and you'll have a fully formed version of your Olympic-gold-medal-level professional event.

A PSA on Defining Your Niche

So far, you've been working on discovering the puzzle *pieces*. Now you're going to be asked to *solve* the puzzle. If you haven't finished the previous steps of the process yet, then please do not move forward. It would be a fool's errand to try to complete a puzzle without all of its pieces. I've seen too many people try to determine their niche without a complete set of information. It is frustrating and ultimately futile. You'll be able to complete most of the puzzle so you'll see a portion of the vision. Then you'll notice one or two missing pieces, which will tempt you to declare the entire process a failure. You deserve better than that. Don't fall victim to this classic mistake.

I know you want clarity. I know you've thrown your hands up in the air and shouted to whoever would listen that you just want to know already. That you'll do anything to know. That you don't even care what it is, you just want all to be revealed! I've been there. But I've also tried to make my square professional peg fit in a round career hole when I was too proud or impatient to go through all the necessary steps. I ended up worse off for it. While you might feel like you're accomplishing something in the short term by skipping steps, in the long term you will be cheating yourself. Not only will you have a less-than-ideal vision, but you'll also be right back where you started. It ain't fun. So, don't do it.

An Example for the Ages

Remember Patricia, the stylist and curator of custom boxes who was about ready to give up when she came to the Nth Degree? She's graciously put herself on display here so that you can learn from her niche-crafting process as a model to do this on your own. In this section, we'll use her example to show you just how robust your three circles—Now, Nature, and Nurture—need to be. In the next chapter, we'll explore her example in greater depth to see how these puzzle pieces actually fit together to create her professional Niche.

We'll begin with her Now step and her core values:

Faith
Family
Connection
Depth
Creativity
Balance
Adventure
Authenticity
Curiosity

Remember, your core values are only as good as your commitments. For brevity, I've shared a few examples of her commitments related to her top core values here:

Family: My family is my joy so I channel my dreams/desires as needed (no working on nights or weekends, and much flexibility needed).

Depth: Go beyond surface level. Support through deep connection to help thrive. Think stitches not bandages.

Authenticity: Exist in alignment with truth. Being open and vulnerable and sharing unlocks potential because I know it's there.

During the Nature step, Patricia gained some critical insights.

Predictive Index: "Promoter" pattern

Myers-Briggs/16 Personalities: ENFP, also called the Campaigner

HIGH5/StrengthsFinder: Empathizer, Storyteller, Coach, Deliverer, and Believer

Interpersonal Mirror: open, sharing, flexibility, commander, mama bear, big picture, connection, expression, leads in ambiguity, persuasive, conviction, and authority.

You may already see some overlap in Patricia's Now and Nature. That's great! Again, resist the urge to make premature assumptions or conclusions. The same will happen when you complete this exercise.

In her Nurture section, she included another robust list of her knowledge, skills, and relative expertise:

Exploration
Curiosity
Performance
Public speaking/articulate
Teaching to teachable people
People in transition with uncertainty or lack of stability
Aware (college students, high school seniors)

Mapping out steps
Enriching lives
Abstract (excited by unknown)
Travel
Undercurrent of excitement
Stability/safety to take risk
People come to me
Subject matter that matters
Service

This level of detail may seem light to you or it may feel like an overwhelming amount to synthesize. Try not to be so hard on yourself. The goal here is to get all of your major insights from the preceding exercises in one place, so you can evaluating them fairly.

Curious how this worked out for Patricia? The punchline in her story is that through the process of discovering her Now, Nature, and Nurture, we not only saved her and her family $70,000 (which she was planning on spending on tuition) but also ten years of her life she would have spent pursuing a less-than-ideal career. In the next chapter, I'll show you how to get the same powerful insight for yourself.

BECOME UNSTOPPABLE:
PUT THE PUZZLE PIECES TOGETHER

Step 1: Gather all your information from the Now, Nature, and Nurture exercises.

Everything you've done so far has been designed to prepare you for this. We're moving from discovering to defining, so you'll need all those puzzle pieces handy to take your first stab at solving the puzzle. Gather:

Insights from Now: core values, commitments, vision
Insights from Nature: assessments, mirror exercise feedback
Insights from Nurture: education, work experience, ninja skills

Step 2: Create your Venn diagram.

On a very large piece of paper (or in a digital/visual document), create three large overlapping circles to form your niche framework. Following the diagram on page 131, label the large circles Now, Nature, and Nurture. The goal here is to collect everything you've discovered in the *same place* for simultaneous review (we don't want to leave out any of that discovery work!).

Step 3: Fill in the circles.

Transfer the information from your exercises into the appropriate circles. Include any relevant insights from each step in the process thus far. For your Now circle, the minimum viable amount of information are your core values and commitments. For your Nature circle, include your behavioral assessment results and the traits identified by your mirror exercise participants. In the Nurture circle, include educational, professional, and life experiences and what you want to stretch toward.

Step 4: Review.

Look at your diagram and make sure that you've recorded any relevant insights from the earlier sections of this book. Going forward, you will fill out the rest of the diagram, and while you can keep adding to Now, Nurture, and Nature as you go along, it is ideal to start with everything at your disposal.

"You gotta keep trying to find
your niche and trying to fit into
whatever slot that's left for you or
to make one of your own."

DOLLY PARTON

THE NEXUS OF NOW, NATURE, AND NURTURE

YOU'VE FINALLY REACHED the point at which you can begin to make some inferences and conclusions about your career based on all the work you've done so far. Now, in a step-by-step fashion, you're going to find out how all these insights align and overlap to illuminate your ideal professional pursuit. The easiest way to do this systematically is by using your commitments as a compass. One by one, examine how each commitment overlaps with your insights in Nature and your insights in Nurture, until you have a complete list of requirements for and components of your professional niche. This will represent all the qualities you need in your ideal dream job.

When I first set out to write this book, I had a startling realization. In one breath, I was saying how we never really succeed on our own and we desperately need mentors and coaches to get to the next level, especially in our career. Then, just a couple of chapters later, I was writing a step-by-step process to, theoretically, complete the niche-crafting process alone. Already, more than once, I've prompted you to reach out for help or consult your network. It's absolutely necessary to incorporate the positive opinions of others when you have a hard time seeing the best version of yourself. Similarly, to do my job well, I must share another insight with you and encourage you to take it. While I am confident that you are smart and could do this process reasonably well on your own, the niche-crafting process is *always* easiest with help.

Remember the PSA from my business coach about doing open-heart surgery on yourself? You can have all the information and experience you need, but if you lack the proper perspective, guidance, and objectivity, the process can get messy fast. You'll likely struggle to get the outcome you expect, especially the first time you complete the niche-crafting process. It would be unfair for me to not prepare you for this reality. There is no replacement for a coach, mentor, or insightful friend to complete the next step with you. I'm not saying you can't give it a go yourself. In fact, I'd highly encourage you to try this on your own *first*. But I would hate for you to struggle through this process alone and give up because of confusion, overwhelm, or frustration. In my experience, this process is best completed with the help of a coach, mentor, advisor, or trusted friend.

Your Career Mathematical Equation

To define your niche, you're going to do some "career math": you'll take your core values and commitments (Now); align them with your personality, behaviors, and gifts (Nature); and see where that combination overlaps with your learned skills, knowledge, and expertise (Nurture). The goal is to arrive at *components* of your ideal professional niche—the "big picture," so to speak.

As you can imagine, this process is more of an art than a science. However, you can keep it "mathematical" and make tackling this process easier by using a logical order. Start by

Consider getting support as you clarify your niche. After all, if you could figure it out on your own, you would have by now.

reading your number-one core value and its accompanying commitment. Ask yourself where this value and commitment overlap with insights you've discovered about your Nature. Then ask yourself how that same value/commitment overlaps with insights discovered in Nurture. The last step is to record these collective insights as a component of your Niche. Go through this process for each value/commitment. Voila! You have a niche.

The results of this process look different for everyone. For instance, two people with similar Now and Nurture but different Nature will have very different outputs. Let's say they both want to dedicate their careers to basketball. Because of a different in Nature, it might be viable for one to become an announcer while the Nature of the other leads them to becoming a player. It's important to remember that this process was meant to target your ideal and nothing less. You're shooting for the moon, not the stars. We've been taught to hold back, or believe we're asking for too much or not keeping enough of an open mind. If I've learned one thing from all my years of working on careers, it's this: there exists, for each of us, an ideal career that doesn't require you to sacrifice *anything* that matters to you. This ideal career will empower you to become the best professional version of yourself. Period. You've come too far to settle for anything less.

Our Niche Example, Continued

Again, to simplify the process, attack niche defining by starting with your top value and commitment and then connect the dots between it and your discoveries from Nature and Nurture to arrive at one aspect of your niche. To demonstrate, let's bring Patricia back into the picture. I'll take you through her niche-crafting process, beginning with a core value and commitment then ending with a key component of her professional niche.

Now

Patricia's third core value: Connection

Her commitment surrounding connection: Heart to God, hand to man. As a conduit of love to community, I enrich the lives of others.

Overlap with Nature

Predictive Index—"Promoter" pattern: Promoters naturally make connections with others.

Myers-Briggs/16 Personalities—ENFP (also called the Campaigner): ENFPs have a giftedness for persuasion and engagement.

HIGH5/StrengthsFinder—Empathizer: Empathy is a natural way to make human connection. Coach: This is a specific way to make a connection to another person.

Interpersonal Mirror—Mama bear and connection.

Overlap with Nurture

Connection as a value and her natural abilities as a connector from her assessments also overlapped with her Nurture in the following areas:

Performance
Public speaking/articulate
Teaching to teachable people
Interest in helping people in transition with uncertainty or lack of stability
Enriching lives
Abstract (excited by unknown)
People come to me

Niche conclusion

In her own words, Patricia came up with this component of her Niche based on how connection overlapped with her Nature and Nurture: "Supporting other people through deep connection to help them thrive."

This component of Patricia's Niche clearly includes connection. It demonstrates how she can use her Nature (empathy, coaching, and engagement) to live the value of connection in her work. It also shows how she can leverage insights from her Nurture (teaching, working through uncertainty, and enriching lives) to ensure her work focuses on connection. Beautiful!

It's finally your turn to step up to the plate. Embrace the art of this process by using the structure I've recommended. Simply choose one core value and its commitment, see where that overlaps with both your Nature and Nurture, and draw a simple conclusion about how this will become or relate to a component of your Niche—work that is *ideal*. If you're really stressing and find yourself putting too much pressure on this step, know you are not the first! I find it's best to approach this exercise as a rough draft of your final niche. Think of it as the big picture rather than the minutiae of a particular job or requirements of a certain role. Remember your niche is a *zone* of genius, not a singular job. In the next chapter, we will go into more detail and define your precise next step. For now, embrace your overall zone of genius. Get ready for your vision for the future to reveal itself, one core value and commitment at a time.

BECOME UNSTOPPABLE!
YOUR NICHE-CRAFTING PROCESS

Step 1: Follow the niche discovery process.

Beginning with your number-one core value and its accompanying commitment, ask yourself out loud:

"How does this commitment overlap with my Nature?"
"How does this same commitment overlap with my Nurture?"
Finally, "What facet of my Niche does this overlap highlight?"

Record your answer in the niche section at the center of the diagram.

Step 2: Repeat until complete.

Repeat step 1 for each of your core values and commitments, in their order of importance. When you're done, you'll have one component of your niche for each of your core values. Each niche statement may look and feel theoretical, but that's the point. You're identifying your ideal genius zone. The next step is defining exactly *where* you will play in that sandbox. We'll do that by embracing this broader vision and giving it more detail and reality.

"The truth of the story
lies in the details."

PAUL AUSTER

GIVE YOUR VISION
THE NECESSARY DETAILS

Y NOW, YOU'VE done quite a bit of work. Kudos to you! You've determined your life circumstances, core values, and commitments. You've assessed your gifts and talents and defined your personality and behaviors. You've uncovered your accumulated knowledge, skills, and expertise. Most recently, you've taken insights from all this discovery to define a list of attributes of your niche—your professional genius zone. You've put in more work than most people are willing to do and you're on the road to results that most people will never get. This is an *incredible* accomplishment that needs to be celebrated as such. So please, in the name of all that is good, give yourself a well-deserved pat on the back. Or pop champagne. That's my preference. But whatever works for you!

But now you may be thinking, "Well, Tracy, I have this list of components that make up my professional niche, but it still doesn't make sense to me. It feels vague . . . now what? How do I find a job in the real world? What's the job title? Who hires for it? What does it pay? Where does it exist? *Does it exist?!* Help!"

Does it feel like I'm in your brain? If that's a scary "yes," it's because your reaction is like that of every one of our students.

There's a short way and a long way to address these questions. The short way is this: stop it! You have not come this far and done this much work to fall into overwhelm and despair. The long answer is: you're only partway done. I've devised a way to clarify your niche, so it looks and feels more tangible in a professional context. Now we will take this vision of yours and give it detail.

Your Niche in Professional Terms

What you might notice is that your niche—although 100 percent accurate and authentic to you—might not make perfect sense to another person. (Also possible: it barely makes sense to you!) For instance, "complete and total locational freedom" is one thing and "working for myself" is another. Knowing the difference requires more detail about the physical manifestation of your ideal professional vision. Your task now is to translate each component of your niche into language that describes an aspect of a professional work environment. The easiest way to do this is to explore the six Ws we've used before: who, what, when, where, why, and how.

Even though your niche can readily be described by the components you listed in the previous chapter's exercise, it needs to be translated into terminology that other people understand and *envision*. This becomes more crucial as we transition to the next phase, Drive, where you will begin your career search. Tangible definitions also come in handy if you can't help yourself from looking at job boards, or you want to do some career research online. Ultimately, sharing your vision with real, live human beings is your best bet (which we cover later), but sometimes it's impossible to avoid LinkedIn.

Your next exercise is to go through each of the six Ws to help define your dream job and translate your niche from vague vision to clear vocation. Here are some example questions for each of the Ws to get you started:

Who: Who do you work with? Who do you work for? Who are your clients? Who does your work help? Who are you surrounded by on a daily basis? Who do you have a drive to serve?

What: What's the subject matter of your work? What do you physically do day to day? What is your job/role? What is required of you? What does success look like? What is the goal of your work?

When: When do you work? When are your regular hours (if any)? When can you label something done? When do you take vacation? When do you see your family? When are you available and when are you off the grid?

Where: Where do you do your work? Where do you live? Where do you commute or do you at all? Where are your other coworkers (if any)? Where are you expected to be most days? Where does your job require you to travel? Where do you see yourself?

Why: Why do you work? Why do you *do what you do*? Why does your job exist? Why does your company/organization exist? Why do you get up in the morning? Why is the world better because of what you do?

How: How do you deliver your value? How do you get work done? How do you provide service? How do you change lives? How does your company/job make money? How do you define success? How do you achieve sustainability?

Lasting success means continuously challenging your preconceived notions of the world—and of work itself—to truly live the life of your dreams.

After you answer these questions, and others like them, you will have incredible specificity about the kind of work you want to do. You'll have taken a conceptual definition of your dream job and turned it into a realistic description of your ideal career. This step is crucial in creating motivation for yourself and a vision to share with the world. Without it, you'll continue to live in the world of possibility, never having shifted to exploring real-world opportunity.

Let's Get Real

As I've mentioned before, a large (and necessary) part of the Nth Degree process is unlearning: shedding the limiting beliefs and expectations that were set upon you by society, by family, and oftentimes by yourself. This. Is. Not. Easy. It's a process of personal mastery that requires you to challenge your tightly held beliefs about how the world works. For now, trust that there is a better way to think about work. A fully aligned and authentic way. If your professional life has existed below your potential level, then the process of challenging your mindset will take time.

A large part of my current job is conversations. Breakfasts, lunches, strategy sessions, and enrollment calls that take place throughout the day and sometimes into the evening. Although this might sound great ("I'd *love* to get paid to eat breakfast and lunch at restaurants..."), when I started, I struggled to view this as legitimate work. My years at the bank had taught me that if you're not at your desk, you're not doing your job. So, for the first couple of years (yes, years!), I never felt like I was working hard enough. Every day felt like failure, because I had defined a successful day by the number of hours at a desk, not the work accomplished. I could plainly see why this was the case by rewinding to my years on the trading floor. My success or failure was determined by the trades, and trades were determined by desk time. Spending twelve hours in the same chair was simply what successful people did.

Fast-forward to beginner-entrepreneur Tracy conducting sales conversations and strategy meetings over lunch and happy hour. If I didn't close a massive deal in the span of one meeting, I thought of myself as a failure and beat myself up for leaving the office. I didn't take breaks. I ate at my desk when I didn't have meetings. I worked nonstop so that I felt good about the effort I had given that day. It took almost three years for me to unlearn my definition of career success and start giving myself a break. I *was* working hard. In some ways I was working harder than I ever worked before. And this was true even when the fruits of my labor were not immediate or my work was away from the desk. While I had determined that my freedom was massively important to professional niche, I really had to work to own my vision.

Shorten your learning curve by learning from me. Your concept of success will not shift overnight. Your ability to think outside the career box will not turn on like a light switch simply because you defined your niche. The only way to turn your dream into reality is to believe that it is possible, and that it is possible for *you*. Start there. Continue to take baby steps forward. And never, ever look back. Use this opportunity to create an ideal picture of your professional life, and start to embrace it as though it were already happening.

BECOME UNSTOPPABLE: THE SIX WS

Step 1: List the six Ws, and investigate them.
Ask the six W questions (who, what, when, where, why, and how) for each of your niche insights. Not every question will apply to each insight. Don't worry about that. Simply focus on creating a more tangible vision of your ideal professional context.

Step 2: Practice owning this reality by envisioning yourself doing this type of work.
This step is the beginning of a process. The goal: to slay your limiting-belief dragons. How long it will take: impossible to know. Here are a couple of strategies I use with clients whose ability to imagine something ideal gets blocked by their current concept of reality:

> **Envision yourself living in your niche.** Read through your Niche components and your six W answers. Close your eyes and imagine this vision being your reality. Imagine yourself getting ready in the morning, the start of your workday, and the time spent throughout it. Imagine the results of your work. Imagine conversations you would have. The more you can see it in your mind's eye, the more you can believe not only that it's possible but that it's inevitable.

> **Do a little research.** Out of all of history, we are living in the moment when your dream job could be a reality. We have never had more options than we do now. Remember that underwater basket weaver or the frog blogger in Tahiti? These days, if you can imagine it, you can become it, as cheesy

as that may sound. The more you own your vision and seek out examples of others already living it, the more real it will become. Google is the bare minimum. Research is best done by having great conversations with real human beings!

PART THREE

DRIVE

"Sometimes, idealistic people
are put off the whole business
of networking as something tainted
by flattery and the pursuit of selfish
advantage. But virtue in obscurity
is rewarded only in Heaven. To
succeed in this world you have
to be known to people."

SONIA SOTOMAYOR

THE FIRST STEP
IN YOUR SEARCH

THERE I WAS, sitting in a confessional, dumbfounded. I had gone to confession, not because I had been particularly naughty but because, in 2012, confession had also become my free therapy. I'd begin with the proper ritual, then I'd wrap up my session with how anxious and miserable I felt. I had no idea where my life or my career was going. One particular Sunday during my not-so-subtle therapy session, I'd laid all my fears out on the table. My biggest question? Would I ever know who or what I wanted to be? I got an answer, but certainly not the one I was expecting. The priest said, "Yes, there's peace in knowing. Once you know what you want to do, you'll have a real sense of relief. Enjoy that when it happens. But remember knowing is only half the battle. Once you know, you must go and do."

Go and do?! Crap. I had been so myopically focused on not knowing the "what" that I had completed forgotten there would be a "how." I had no earthly idea what I wanted to be "when I grew up" so I hadn't considered what would be required of me when I could finally answer that question. In fact, not knowing was almost a comfortable excuse *not* to go and do. Maybe, deep down, you share that feeling too.

You're somewhere in the transition between "I don't know" and "I know." Hopefully that means you're ready to do what's required to turn that vision into a reality. Empowered with the knowledge of where, how, and for whom you add value, you are now commissioned, in a sense, to do what it takes to get there. But how? Information is power, yes. But information is *not* a strategy.

Simply knowing what you were made for, what you love, where you add value, and who you have a desire to serve isn't enough, although it will feel like a short-term relief. You need a proven, practical, effective strategy to make your vision your career. You now have your niche—your Olympic event. Soon, you'll learn how to articulate that niche with confidence, clarity, and certainty. But how do you get there? In the Discover phase, we uncovered your true value. In the Define phase, we specified your unique niche. In the final phase of the Nth Degree strategy called Drive, we will put those insights into action so you can drive your dream career into reality.

Getting Back in the Driver's Seat

The Drive phase of the Nth Degree includes three important steps: Network, Navigate, and Nourish. The Network step teaches you vital professional communication strategies and how to leverage the power of people that work in today's marketplace. The Navigate step teaches you simple and practical ways to test your career vision before going all in. The Nourish step prepares you for the journey ahead by equipping you with the necessary motivation and support for a successful career search.

The goal of the Drive phase is to learn actionable tactics to land the job of your dreams faster than you ever imagined possible. While I don't think any of these tactics are particularly novel, I do believe you'll be surprised about where we will begin. Societally, we've been programmed when it comes to career transitions. If I surveyed 100 people and asked where they would start a new job search, the answers are pretty predictable. I'll prove it to you. If I had to bet, I'm guessing your initial reaction upon clarifying your niche was to do one of the following:

Update your résumé
Reformat your LinkedIn profile
Research your niche online
Scroll through job boards (you know you did this!)
Read Glassdoor reviews
Write cover letters
Pray for a headhunter to contact you...

Am I right? Be honest.

The job market has taught us that these kinds of activities are the fastest way to gain traction in a job search. But in the five years I've spent working on careers, I can tell you, unequivocally, that these old-school tactics are not the fastest route to your dream. Sometimes these activities are both useful and vital, especially if you're pursuing a corporate career. However, most of the time for most people, they become a willing distraction rather than actually creating traction. In the Drive phase, I'm going to ask you to go on a journey with me to explore the untapped resources all around you. Whether you believe it or not, there are valuable career assets vying for your attention. These are the people in your life ready and waiting to help you find and land the job of your dreams. I am of the belief that despite our increasingly digital world, your career search must start with exploring the existing value of the people around you. When you leverage their unmatched collective genius, you can leapfrog the tradition job search and uncover a completely hidden job market. But first, we need to get a couple of misconceptions out of the way about the word "network" and what it means to leverage the power of people.

Redefining the Job Search

What comes to mind when you think about the term "career search"? Chances are, after shuddering, you start to think about all of your assets *you* need to identify, apply for, and interview for to secure a new job. Perhaps you envision countless hours updating your résumé, scrolling job boards, and completing digital applications. While this approach is absolutely logical, it lacks one important aspect for speed: leverage. There's only so much you can do alone. In this approach, your progress is limited by the time and attention you can afford to give to the job search. But what if there were more brains than yours working on this problem?

You have a choice here. You can slog through the career search process *alone* hoping to be discovered by a recruiter or have your dream position jump off the screen on a job board. I stubbornly tried that for a long time. The more pressure I put on myself to figure this out, the more isolated and defeated I became. It wasn't until I tapped into my network that my search started to show real progress. Once I shared my vision for the future (no matter how half-baked), I opened myself to receive feedback and guidance from people who knew more than me. Once I embraced these mentors and committed to growing a network of dedicated career advocates, I finally made progress toward my *ideal* career.

If you still need convincing and can't shake the dread that creeps into your stomach when you think about going to a stuffy networking event and handing out business cards, I get it! That's how our society characterizes networking. But it's not the only way. As an incentive to challenge this mindset, consider this: studies cited by *Business Insider*, NPR, *Forbes*, PayScale, LinkedIn, and countless recruiting blogs show the stunning power of people. It's a verified fact that anywhere between 70 to 85 percent of jobs are found by networking.[8] That's not a typo... 75 to 80 percent! The craziest part? According to these same studies, the vast majority of jobs (up to 80 percent) are not even *listed*. In other words, by not prioritizing the power of people, we're missing out on 70 to 85 percent of the opportunities. Networking rewards the job seeker because business is all about *people*.

The Hidden Job Market

The practical implication of this statistic is one undeniable fact: the larger, more dynamic job market is fundamentally *hidden*. According to one study, only 15 to 30 percent of *all possible jobs* are identified through some sort of commonplace methodology—online applications, recruiters, résumé wars, and the like. The overwhelming majority of new and newly open roles are never even posted. If these roles are posted, these studies prove that effective networkers secure these roles more often. Sorry to be the bearer of bad news, but those hours we've all spent trolling Indeed postings and LinkedIn opportunities were most likely in vain. It seems that while these activities make us *feel* busy, they aren't really moving the needle in our search. Regardless of how you feel about networking, you'd be foolish to deny the facts. The hidden job market shows exactly why identifying, leveraging, and building a strong network is so important.

But what is networking, really? I believe that we've generalized the concept of networking as something icky, like it's a used-car-salesman approach to finding a job. Imagine a cramped and poorly lit conference room full of people shaking hands, aggressively and disinterestedly asking that dreaded question, "So, what do you do?" I love people, but even I hate events like that. When you assume all networking looks like this unsavory scenario, it's enough to make you shudder and give up before you even begin.

Not a Four-Letter Word

Networking does not have to be the hellish scene I've described above. I've been to plenty of those horrendous events. Trust me, they are about as good a use of your time as scrolling through the interwebs and hoping your dream job falls in your lap.

True networking—the kind that advances careers and creates lifelong, professional, sponsor-based relationships—doesn't happen that way. You don't have to force yourself into a scenario where each party is trying to get something out of the other. True networking happens when two like-minded, respectful individuals *collaborate*. It happens when you're in line at the grocery store and you happen to have the same items as the person in front of you. It happens when you're on the plane sitting next to a total stranger and you decide to chat instead of immediately putting on headphones. It happens when you go to a shower or party or wedding and share your career vision with an old friend. Turns out, she knows someone who knows exactly the type of work you're looking for, and they'd be happy to talk to you about it further over coffee. *That* is networking. It's all around us and it's available all the time.

Recently, I met some friends at a bar to watch college football, and outside the front door was a sign that read "3D Tinder, Come Inside!" I laughed so hard when I realized what it was saying: we've replaced real, live networking—a.k.a. interfacing with other human beings—with electronics and apps. We hide behind our technology. We've become a shy, awkward population who use our devices as shields so we won't feel exposed or rejected in real life. The bar environment *was* 3D Tinder! It was a not-so-subtle reminder that we have the opportunity to meet people outside of the digital barriers we've created. There's no better reason than a career transition to test this out in your own life.

I believe the internet has done amazing things for our society, but reliance on digital engagement has impacted our ability to *physically* meet and interact with other human beings. We think our career problems can be solved from the comfort of the couch or at the touch of our fingertips. But when the data show that 70 to 85 percent of the jobs out there are being nabbed by those willing to get out of the house and interact with other human beings, we're missing the boat! So, if you're one of those people who's always thought that networking was as foul as a four-letter word, I hope you will trust the math and give this a shot.

Think about your odds here: if so few of us are willing to reach out and network effectively on our own behalf, *plus* the overwhelming majority of jobs are won by those who engage with others, then you have a unique opportunity. You can be the 20 percent taking advantage of 80 percent of the opportunities. It's just like sales, in a way. They say that the average sale takes twelve or more instances of contact, or touchpoints, before a deal is made. Data also shows that the vast majority of salespeople (approximately 80 percent) give up after just three to four attempts. That means the majority of the sales (80 percent) go to the 20 percent of salespeople willing to put in the extra effort.[9] Make Pareto proud. Leverage this advantage as you begin the search for your ideal career.

Win by Doing What No One Else Will Do

If you embrace the concepts in Network, you'll be able to advance your career search faster with three major assets:

1 An elevator pitch that will knock socks off.
2 A solid understanding of how and when to ask for help.
3 A proven strategy for building and nurturing your network.

In the chapters ahead, we're going to look at each of these vital components to accelerate your career search. But first, I'd like to debunk the most common ~~excuse~~ objection I hear when it comes to leveraging the power of people in your job search. Nearly every client I've had says that they "don't know anyone" or they have already "completely tapped" their existing networks. Or my personal favorite: networking "just doesn't work" for them.

My client Mary was unconvinced about networking. Her whole career had been in digital design, so to her it made sense to remain in her medium while searching for her dream job. I told Mary that she didn't need to be convinced about networking but encouraged her to give it a try. At my direction, Mary reached out to five people in her existing network. She considered them longshots to help her. They either lived a great distance away, she hadn't contacted them in years, or they had senior titles and very little time for socializing.

Before she reached out, Mary and I worked together to create a masterful pitch—a way to share her request, transition, and journey that would encourage the person to help (you'll get one of these in a chapter or two!). We also crafted a plan for what to say when she got an in-person meeting.

What happened next *seemed* miraculous, but it was really just the 20 percent taking advantage of the 80. Mary reached out to all five of these contacts via email with the script we had created. One man, who lived out of town, wrote back that he was traveling for business and could meet *that day* for lunch. Despite her hesitation that she wasn't "ready" for such a meeting, I encouraged Mary to take advantage of this serendipitous opportunity. She canceled her preexisting plans, met him for lunch, explained her situation, and shared her vision for her career using a crafted in-person pitch. She was looking to transition from full-time employment into freelancing and consulting in a similar line of business. As she described her value, vision, and desire, something incredible happened that she never expected: his response was "I think I have some work for you."

Turns out he was looking for someone to provide the *exact* value she promised for a new project. Not only that, but he wanted that talent on contract rather than someone to come on full-time. Less than one week later, Mary found herself hired on as a self-employed contractor. She was in business almost before she had started!

Mary's results are not unique. Sure, it was a great and well-timed opportunity, but it wasn't an *accident*. She reached out to the right person, said the right things, showed up in the right way, and bang! Career success! As with Mary's example, the easiest place to begin networking is with your preexisting contacts. It's honestly that simple. Most people hear the word "network" and immediately picture reaching out total strangers and asking for favors. That's a fear-based response. When we let fear call the shots, we envision certain activities as much harder than they need to be. Why not keep it simple and start by networking with the people who already know, like, and trust you and who would love the opportunity to help?

Auditing Your Current Network

Your present network is a precious and dear commodity. These people represent the surest path to career clarity and success.

You're going to start with your current, immediate network (a.k.a. people you already know): your parents, your siblings, your close friends, your colleagues, your professors or advisors, your mentors. All the people you've made part of your inner circle along the road of life. This amazing resource of people who believe in you is just waiting to be tapped. Breathe a sigh of relief: you don't have to go to a networking event tomorrow and pitch yourself to a room full of strangers. Start with who you know, and go from there.

From the first time we used the word "network," Teresa resisted. She was convinced that her niche—serving victims of human trafficking—was so specific and narrow that networking would never work for her (plus she was nervous about sharing her vision with total strangers). I encouraged her to lean outside her comfort zone, to simply look at her current network to see who could help. Doing so, she identified two former colleagues who could become advocates (more about that in the next section). Her opportunity for growing her network (more on this in the next section as well) also became clear. She knew plenty of people who directly served victims, but very few who worked for the companies who supported those direct-service organizations. Suddenly, what started out as overwhelming ("I have to connect with the entire world of human-trafficking prevention") became very simple ("I have to connect with consulting firms that support service organizations"). Her best bet at growing her network strategically was to connect with more people who empowered those who served. She went from confused to clear, knowing exactly who she needed to meet.

Begin by creating a quick but comprehensive list of the people in your network who could become career advocates. Having a clear "inventory" of your existing network will be valuable when you do eventually start expanding your reach. For example, if you do a network inventory and realize that everyone in your inner circle is in the same industry, then perhaps that's an opportunity to grow your network's diversity. Try not to overwhelm yourself doing this. I'm not asking you to note every person you know. But I do want you to look objectively at your current network and identify the diamonds in the rough.

Start with the closest and most obvious people. You might not have to go much further than that, if you're lucky. But keep going in wider and wider spheres of influence, and you'll no doubt find a colleague, advisor, or long-lost friend who might have the answers or opportunity you need. Then you're going to begin to draw conclusions as to how these relationships can support you in the pursuit of your niche.

BECOME UNSTOPPABLE:
YOUR CURRENT NETWORK

Step 1: Brainstorm a list of your current network.

As a quick primer, this list can include, but does not need to be limited to, the following:

Immediate family
Extended family (aunts, uncles, cousins, and so on)
Current friends
Childhood/high school/college personal contacts
Childhood/high school/college professional contacts
Mentors/coaches/sponsors/advisors
Current and previous colleagues

Step 2: Compare this list to your niche and its needs.

By this point, you've got some sense of your niche. If you're still looking for clarity (a job title, specific industry, role requirements), then the first purpose that your network can serve is help clarify your vision. Scan your list for the people you know would be most helpful in nailing down some details within your vision.

If you are clear about your niche, think about the next purpose your network can serve. Do you need an introduction to someone specific? Do you need to learn something about your vision? Do you need support or motivation from anyone? Scan your list and begin to connect the dots between what you need and who would best provide that service for your career. Define a specific purpose for each relationship you listed.

Step 3: Go further back.

Take a moment to realize that any given person on your list, unless you've known them from birth, was at one point added to your network. Perhaps you met them without an intermediary, but more than likely, you were introduced to the majority of the people on your list by *other* people also on your list. Embrace this fact. Trace your relationship with each individual back to the person who introduced you. Keep going until you reach an organic meeting, one that wasn't facilitated by another person. Use this brainstorming activity not for any specific outcome but to prove to yourself how powerful networking can be. Relationships, friends, businesses, and careers all move the fastest and most efficiently when you go through people to get where you want to go.

"The purpose of an elevator pitch
is to describe a situation or solution so
compelling that the person you're
with wants to hear more even after
the elevator ride is over."

SETH GODIN

PREPARE TO SHARE
YOUR VISION

IMAGINE THIS: YOU'RE at the grocery store, minding your own business and contemplating the merits of cauliflower rice when you run into your old boss. You loved this guy and he always just seemed to "get" you. It's been years since you've caught up with him, so he stops and asks you what you're up to these days. Naturally the conversation leads to career, and all of a sudden you're on the spot. It's showtime.

This is the *perfect* opportunity to engage in some unexpected strategic networking. Based on what you share with him, you could have one of those amazing, serendipitous conversations that opens your eyes to a new opportunity. This could be the missing link between the limbo you're in now and finally being happy doing something that you absolutely love. You could be one step closer to a job that takes advantage of where you are, what you like, and what you've learned over the years. Living and working in your niche. Hallelujah!

Except you have a problem. When he asks what you're up to and you open your mouth, nothing comes out. Or worse, something awful and disorganized spills out. "Well, I have this new job that I really hate, and I'm trying to figure out what I want to do, and I'm just not sure yet, but I think it has something to do with this niche thing that I just created. Any chance you know of anyone who's hiring? Could you look at my résumé?"

Cue confused, overwhelmed, well-meaning ex-boss politely saying, "Not really, but hey, it's great to see you. I'll keep you in mind," and promptly running away from the produce aisle.

The Importance of Preparing a Pitch

Putting together coherent thoughts under pressure is tough, even for those who know exactly what they want to say! Extemporaneous speaking is even harder if you haven't taken the time to organize your thoughts in the first place. You must prepare for this type of in-the-moment scenario so that you can take advantage of any opportunity to leverage or expand your network. Keeping an elevator pitch about your ideal career in your back pocket is vital. An elevator pitch is a short, prepared, targeted statement that, in this case, explains where you are in life, what you're looking for next, and how someone can help you. The next time you run into an opportunity like the one above, if you want something other than passing well wishes, then a practiced pitch is exactly what you need.

Take a tip from me: please don't skip this step. I've done enterprise and direct sales and professional speaking for the majority of my adult working life, so I've spoken off the cuff plenty of times. Yet even I screw this up sometimes. I'll be at a random event, and someone will catch me off guard with an annoying "So, what do you do?" If I'm not already in networking mode, sometimes my mind goes completely blank and I trip over my words. I had to prepare and practice an explanation of who I am, what I do, how I deliver value, and why that matters. Otherwise, I would blurt out something general and incoherent that wouldn't get me any closer to my goals.

In networking conversations, people listen for key words and concepts they can identify to put you into context. The brain needs a box in which to place you. That's why the question "What do you do?" can be such a conversation killer. If you don't have relatable or relevant information for them, then they put you into the "not relevant to me" brain file. The conversation is over. You know that's happened when you get the dreaded "I'll keep you in mind" reaction, which is the kiss of death for networking (ahem, all) conversations. To combat this pitfall, I've taken everything I've learned from sales, speaking, and business to create a simple step-by-step process for writing, practicing, and mastering your career elevator pitch. It looks like this.

Four-Part Career Pitch

1 Purpose: Identify the one goal behind the pitch.
2 Enroll: Use a transition statement to create context.
3 Envision: Describe your ideal career in visual terms.
4 Ask: Create a question that serves the purpose.

Purpose

The first thing you want to do is figure out the *purpose* behind the pitch: what are you trying to accomplish by speaking to this person in the first place? Based on where you are in your career search, what's the next piece of support or information you need? Do you want an introduction? Do you want help clarifying your dream job? Do you want a recommendation? Do you want a job offer? Do you need help figuring out the ideal title for your position? Getting crystal clear on exactly what you want to accomplish with each conversation determines the details you include, the questions you ask, and the positioning you use in your elevator pitch.

Keeping **an elevator pitch about your ideal career** in your back pocket is vital to capitalizing on impromptu networking opportunities.

When you're just starting out in the Network step, you're likely still in need of a little additional clarity. For most of our students, their niche sounds great, but it doesn't necessarily call to mind a specific job or a role with a specific title. That happens because you can't possibly know all the jobs that exist! This result happens all the time and can be extremely frustrating for someone who's put in all the work in Now, Nature, Nurture, and Niche. If your niche has a clear professional manifestation, that's awesome! You're one step ahead, and good for you. However, if your niche sounds like an amazing idea that could still use clarification, then the purpose of your initial networking conversations is to tighten up your niche. These early conversations will help you uncover the potential jobs, roles, industries, and companies that align with your vision.

As you continue having networking conversations, your needs will evolve. Eventually, you'll want help with other ways to progress your job search like introductions, recommendations, mentoring, sponsorship, or interviews. Make sure you're clear about the goal you have in mind for your pitch before you start writing it. Everything else hinges on this clarity of purpose.

Enroll

After you identify your goal—the purpose behind the pitch—you'll be able to start crafting your pitch. The best pitches begin by providing relevant context that enrolls your networking partner in your journey. While the career search is top of mind for you, your networking buddy is hearing this story for the first time. If you fail to provide context for your listener so they understand where you are in the journey, they enter the conversation lost. In sales, they say, "A confused buyer never buys." In networking, I like to say, "A confused listener can't help you." A good opening statement explains where you are in your life, the work you've done to make a change, and sets the stage for pursuing a transition. This opening can be incredibly simple, if you allow it to be. Remember, its only purpose is to provide context. Here are a few examples of opening enrollment statements in two sentences or less:

> "I'm exploring other opportunities outside of my current role. In fact, I've been working through a career clarity process called the Nth Degree, and I'm excited to share my vision for my future career with you."

> "I'm in the midst of a career transition from something I do well to something I really love. I've taken a lot of time to put together a vision for this future career, and I'd love to share that with you to gain some much-needed perspective."

> "I'm making a career transition, and I could really use your help."

Crafting a positive enrollment statement that sets the stage for transition is often a humbling part of this process. None of us want to look like we don't have our act together, so we're tempted to pretend that everything is fine. We also don't want to look like whiners or complainers, so we might even sugarcoat our feelings about the job we're just tolerating or downright hating. Choose an accurate and articulate way to say that you want something new in your career. Simply stating that you've reached a crossroads and you're ready to explore different options is usually enough for people. The goal here is to enroll someone in your process of discovery, so they will be even more excited to support you through the journey. Imagine that the people you're speaking to know nothing about you or your background. Help them get on the same page as you as quickly as possible.

Envision

Once you've written your enrollment statement, then you'll want to start describing your vision for the future. This is your first chance to share your niche! Don't let this be too daunting of a task. Simply summarize all the information you recorded in the Niche section, and share your vision by painting a mental picture for the person who's listening to your pitch. Most importantly, you'll focus exclusively on your ideal future state. Now is not the time to compare your vision with your past or to speak negatively about your current job. You've already enrolled your listener in your journey of transition. Now is the time to give them your hard-earned vision! Let's take this idea for a spin.

> **Instead of saying:** "I'm stuck in a cubicle all day and I hate it and want to do something different, maybe even outdoors."
> **Reframe to a positive vision:** "I really value my physical freedom, I love the outdoors, and I perform at my best away from a desk, so I'm pursuing a mobile or remote role."

> **Instead of saying:** "I'm completely isolated and alone all day, and it's really harming my morale and my productivity."
> **Reframe to a positive vision:** "I add so much value in a group setting where I can collaborate with a community of coworkers face to face, in real time."

> **Instead of saying:** "My boss is a jerk, my team is full of idiots, and I cannot suffer fools."
> **Reframe to a positive vision:** "I cherish time spent around smart people, and my performance is elevated when I'm challenged by people who know more than me."

Although I hope you'd never consider saying something negative about a previous boss or categorizing an entire group of people as idiots out loud, there's an even better reason to stay positive and future-focused. Remember the Baader-Meinhof phenomenon we talked about before? Your listener's brain will focus on what's right in front of it. If you're talking to people about all about the things you don't want in your future job, that's what they'll focus on. So keep it positive and focused on the future. You'll get better results by indicating the type of environment you're looking for rather than bashing the one you're in. This section of your pitch will be the longest, because you're describing what you know about your niche. Share what you know. Own what you don't. The better the picture you can create in the mind of your listener, the more helpful they can be.

Ask

Perhaps the most important part of your elevator pitch is the last part: asking for specific help. The best elevator pitches end with a question that reengages listeners and brings about their part of the conversation—giving feedback and advice. For example, by asking, "Does what I've described sound like a particular role or title in your industry?" you will learn (a) if they were listening at all, (b) if they understood what you said, and (c) whether or not they can help you in your pursuit.

The question for specific help should speak directly to the purpose behind the pitch. If you're connecting with someone in the hopes they can further clarify your niche, then your question needs to speak directly to that need. If you've moved on to needing introductions or a job offer, then your question will change accordingly. Here are a few examples of specific questions based on different purposes:

Purpose: Clarity
Question: "Based on what I've shared with you, could you help me in narrowing this niche down to a specific job title?"

Purpose: Introductions

Question: "Given that you work in the industry I've just described, is there someone on your team who does this exact role who you could introduce me to?"

Purpose: Job opportunity

Question: "Are you aware of an opportunity within your company that fits the vision I've just described?"

This specific question is only the beginning. It should elicit a direct response from your listener but is not meant to be the only question you ask. You're in a conversation, after all! If you've engaged your listener in your journey with context and painted a vivid picture of your niche, then they will likely have clarifying questions that spur on the dialogue. Resist the temptation to act like you know everything. Your role is to learn and listen, not to dominate. Networking conversations are an opportunity for you to gather new information to add to what you already know. If all you do is talk or make assumptions on behalf of the listener, then you won't discover the unknown. Welcome clarifying questions from your listener, so they can have a full and accurate picture of your vision.

The best way to judge whether you've had a fruitful conversation is to count how many next steps you leave with. Yes, you should start by identifying one main purpose, but the truly valuable networking conversations are going to result in many action items or opportunities for follow-up. Regardless of whether you get one piece of advice or twenty tips about perfectly aligned job opportunities, remember this: you do not want to be "kept in mind." Your goal is to walk away with *something specific* you can use to get closer to your dream job. You may want to be mentored, to be coached, to be introduced to two people, to follow up in two weeks—never to be "kept in mind." Know exactly what you'd like to get out of the conversation and *ask* for that before you leave. This part is sometimes the hardest, especially for those of us who don't want to be a burden on others or ask for too many favors. But trust me, these people want to help you. You just need to tell them *how*.

Putting the Pitch Together

Here are a few examples of fully formulated elevator pitches that you can use as templates for your own:

I'm reaching out to you because I'm looking for a specific introduction. [purpose] I've been in a career transition for the past three months. During that time, I've invested in myself, and I'm excited to say that I have a strong and confident vision for my professional future. [enroll] I've identified that my dream job is working in professional organizing. In that role, I can leverage my detail-oriented and service-driven personality, I can live with more freedom and flexibility by creating my own hours, and I can take advantage of my background in sociology to better understand my clients' needs within their homes. [envision] Do you have a contact within the local association of professional organizers who would be open to speaking with someone who's just getting started? [ask]

I'm glad I ran into you today, because I could really use your career advice. [purpose] It's been a while since we've seen each other, so you should know that I'm making a proactive change in my career. I've spent some time working with a career coach, and I've finally discovered my real professional value and defined my ideal career niche. [enroll] As you know, I've been in construction my whole life. I've identified that I perform at my best when I'm both advocating for the client and giving direction to the construction team. I'm starting my own business operating as liaison between clients and general contractors. [envision] I know you've been in business for yourself for twenty years, so could I ask you a few questions about how you got started? [ask]

I'm excited to be connecting with you to update you on my goals and career vision. [purpose] I attended a career clarity workshop last weekend, and I'm excited to say that I walked away with some significant insights. [enroll] Specifically, I've identified an ideal scenario where I continue to deliver value in my full-time position while spending my energy outside business hours on a fashion-based small business. I see these two pursuits working beautifully together so I can have stability and familiarity while still investing in my dream. [envision] Could I meet with you to talk about my goals for next year and restate my commitment to this full-time role? [ask]

Know this about human nature: people in your network want to walk away feeling like they were helpful. By meeting with you, they are demonstrating the commitment, at least for that short period of time, to helping you solve your problem. Don't throw that gift away because you're afraid to ask for what you want. Leave every networking conversation with at least one next step, even if that is simply to follow up within a certain timeframe. If you set meetings with people or even tactfully use your random meet-ups and party conversations wisely, you will be on your way to dream job in no time.

A Note for My Shy Friends

I've taught strategic networking long enough that I've heard every excuse in the book:

"I don't want to be a burden on other people."
"I'm going to wait until my niche is a little clearer."
"I need to do more of my own research before I start talking to people."
"I hate talking about myself."
"I can do this on my own."

If any of the above resonated with you, or if you've been waiting to throw your "but I'm an introvert" card in my face, ask yourself why. Do you really believe this won't work for you, or are you just afraid to do it? Being an introvert or being shy is not a problem. You can be a successful professional and an introvert all at the same time. I'm not asking you to change the fundamentals of who you are or to shout your vision from the rooftops to complete strangers (unless you want to). I'm firmly nudging you to ask for the help that people already want to give you. The only barrier in their way is not yet knowing the specific help you need.

If you don't like talking about yourself but you don't want to waste valuable time on jobs boards, you're going to have to get over that. Life, including your job search, is a constant sales pitch. If you want to succeed, you'll need to be able to articulate your value. This is not self-promotion. It's self-*advocacy*. If you're not a willing advocate and cheerleader for yourself, it's highly unlikely that anyone else will be either. To get comfortable with this idea, practice talking yourself up with friends and family. Ask for their feedback on your pitch. Get comfortable talking about how and who you serve the best! A world of people out there wants to help you. Your job is to tell them exactly how they can do that using your pitch.

BECOME UNSTOPPABLE:
YOUR FIRST PITCH

Step 1: Think strategically about your elevator pitch.
Spend some time considering your niche and what you need, right now, to take the next step toward realizing it. In your workbook, write down:

1 Purpose: the purpose behind the pitch.
2 Enroll: a transition enrollment statement.
3 Envision: your vision for the future.
4 Ask: the specific help you need.

Step 2: Put it all together.
Your purpose, transition statement, vision, and the help you need should each account for one to two sentences in a pitch. Any longer and you're likely going to lose your listener's attention. This pitch can be used either as an initial request for a meeting (in email, for example) or at the outset of the networking conversation itself. Either way, use it to set the stage for a fruitful conversation.

"If you want to go fast, go alone.
If you want to go far, go with others."

PROVERB

MAXIMIZE THE POWER OF PEOPLE

S O FAR IN the Network step of the Nth Degree, we've created a comprehensive list of your current connections and created a tailored pitch for your initial conversations. You're off to a great start leveraging the power of people to accelerate your career search. In this chapter we'll cover the various specific ways you can maximize the help that people can provide.

Empowering Your First Career Advocates

Having a large, positive, diverse, and well-connected network is great. But where do you start? I believe it's incredibly important to identify, appreciate, and empower the handful of individuals who are specially situated to help you forward. I call these individuals your career advocates. These are the people who will take up your cause by performing highly leveraged actions for which they are uniquely suited. This could be a mentor who keeps you motivated through the process, a sponsor who puts your name in the hat for an unlisted opportunity, or a champion who speaks to your value when you're not around. Not every person in your network will be a career advocate. This is a special role reserved for the people who are best positioned to help you get from A to Z, faster than the rest. They are the most relevant. In my professional opinion, there is no better or quicker way to get you where you want to go than with the aid of career advocates.

A small but mighty and passionate group of advocates is all you need to start networking toward your niche. Career advocates are the people uniquely positioned to help. They will likely have the most relevant connections or information for your unique niche. They're the ones who immediately get it when you describe your ideal career to them. They enthusiastically share ideas about the types of jobs or industries where you can apply your expertise. They offer suggestions or introductions at will, without having to be asked. They show a vested interest in your success and want to help you, no matter what it takes. If you sense that someone really wants to help you and perhaps go above and beyond the basic networking conversation or introductions, then ask for what you want from them. Directly. Without mincing words. Here are a few examples:

"Would you be willing to advocate for me and my career?"
"Would you be willing to meet for a follow-up conversation?"
"Would you be willing to offer me support or mentorship?"
"Would you be willing to help me get to the next step in my career?"

Several voices singing the same message are far more effective than you delivering a solo. I know you're committed to leveraging the power of people in your search. Advocates are the key to maximizing this leverage. Actively seek out the people who will be your dedicated advocates going forward. Express your thanks to these people and know that, one day, you will return the favor or pay it forward.

Network-Building Strategies

Once you have a solid list of the people you know who would reasonably be able to help you, you'll probably start to notice where this list is lacking. Like most people, you've likely been gathering people into your network without much deliberation. You were born into your family. You lived with your friends in college, played on teams with them, or happened to meet them through other friends. You sat in a cubicle next to your colleagues; maybe they had similar after-work interests. Your advisors are the professors you bonded with, previous bosses who looked out for you, or mentors you met along the way.

But how many of these relationships were *intentional*? How *proactive* have you been in surrounding yourself with the right kinds of people? Like Jim Rohn said, you're the average of the five people you spend the most time with. Have you chosen those people with purpose? If you're serious about finding work you love and living with more fulfillment and meaning, then you have to be conscious not only about *how* you spend your time but about *who* you spend it with. This is where you'll start to grow your network strategically.

In a famous scene in the 1992 film *Glengarry Glen Ross*, Alec Baldwin's character, Blake, attempts to motivate a sales team to achieve better results. The scene is so iconic that salespeople, traders, and managers still quote it. In addition to being hilariously intense, Blake simplifies the sales process into a couple of initialisms, the most popular of which is A.B.C.—"A: always, B: be, C: closing." When I was thinking about a simple way to articulate my approach to networking, I chose to pay homage to this iconic reference. My A.B.C. method for growing your network, which in many ways is similar to selling, is "A: always, B: be, C: connecting." Always be connecting. Remember the statistic we talked about:

70 to 85 percent of jobs are ultimately acquired through networking. No gesture or amount of influence from another person is too small to advance your career.

You meet new people all the time, but you probably take those random encounters for granted. Sitting next to someone on the train? How about striking up a conversation instead of looking out the window. Waiting for a flight? How about saying hello to the sweet old lady next to you instead of playing on your phone. The universe throws people into your path constantly. It's up to you to take advantage of these natural and organic connections that are likely to happen only once. I met one of my most influential mentors trying to squeeze into a bus in the middle of Cambodia. We talked for all of two minutes in between stops, and it could have ended there. Instead, I followed up with her and asked for her guidance. Because of that serendipitous interaction, my life is completely different, for the better. She taught me the "nothing is wasted" philosophy, among other lessons! This type of opportunity can and will happen to you. If you're open to it and you're vigilant, these otherwise trivial interactions can have life-changing results. Always be connecting.

A.B.C. is a mindset as well as a strategy. As mentioned above, the easiest place to start networking is meeting with people you already know—your career advocates in particular. Once you're ready to move beyond clarity and on to growing your network strategically, you're not going to leave those meetings without directly asking for introductions. I promise you this: unless you ask for introductions directly ("Do you know anyone else who would be helpful to speak with in this situation?"), it's highly unlikely that a person will offer them freely. People want to help but they can be protective of their professional network. By clearly stating that your intention is to learn more about your options by growing your network, you give people an opportunity to share contacts with you.

Be specific in your requests. Do you want to meet someone in a certain industry? Ask for that. A certain profession? Ask for that. Someone with a lot of influence or who might be hiring? Ask for that. Make it easy for the person sitting across from you to know how to be helpful. If you have some particulars already figured out, asking for connections with individuals who meet those requirements will move your search along even faster.

Stare fear in the face and do this anyway. Moving out of your comfort zone to meet with new people and share your deepest vulnerabilities is nothing short of terrifying. I know it was for me! For my whole life, I'd rested on the fact that my experience looked impressive to other people. All As in school, varsity letters in sports, first chair in music... I was on top of the world. But when my world came crashing down at twenty-five and I no longer appeared as shiny as I wanted to be, I struggled to share that with my friends, let alone strangers. To get out of my rut and turn it into a renaissance, I had to build up the courage to share my story and the humility to allow other people to help me.

Your Networking Action Plan

Before you have any networking conversations, even with those advocates, I encourage you to devise a plan. That way, no matter how outgoing or shy you consider yourself to be, you're in control of the conversation. With a plan, you'll have the best chance at getting what you really need.

To begin, you'll want to get comfortable setting clear expectations for your conversation. In the sales world, we call this creating a verbal agenda. This is crucial for one specific reason: no one else is in your head! Remember the people you ultimately meet with will have very little idea what they've gotten themselves into. They haven't yet had the pleasure of going on this transformational journey with you. They'll know you'd like their help and that you're in some kind of transition. Other than that, they're looking for you to fill in the gaps. It's your job to frame the conversation in a way that makes sense to the listener while also being helpful to you. So, rather than launching into the conversation with your pitch and immediately going for the close ("So, can I get an introduction?!"), take a breath. Set the stage for a fruitful conversation with one or two opening lines that show your appreciation and give the conversation a little context. After thanking your networking partner for their time, be prepared with an opening line. These can be as simple as:

"I've always appreciated your advice in the past and could really use your help now."
"I'm so excited to share my current vision for the future and incorporate your advice."

See? Super-easy.

Now they know exactly why they're there, what to listen for, and how they can contribute to the conversation. But this is just the beginning.

Next, you'll want to utilize that pitch we created! Share the specific purpose for the conversation (unless you have already), explain your transition so they are enrolled in your journey, share your positive vision for the future, and then . . . you guessed it . . . ask for help! The most important thing to remember is that you are there to *learn what you don't already know*. As tempting as it may be, do not make assumptions or offer answers on behalf of the listener. You'll be lured to do this because you (a) want to look impressive, (b) feel awkward, or (c) can't stand long pauses (or is that just me?). Don't do it! Let the person think! For instance, if you know what the job sounds like, looks like, and feels like, but have no idea what it's called or if that job exists, *resist the urge to guess or fill in the blanks.* Lean into the long and awkward pause and allow your networking partner time to process what you've said and respond thoughtfully.

The reason this is so important rests in human cognition. Suggesting an answer might activate your listener's confirmation bias. This is a cognitive phenomenon that makes it nearly impossible for someone to offer a unique suggestion. Have you ever heard a muffled song, struggled to figure out what it is, only to have someone yell, "That sounds like the 'Macarena'!"? Drats! Now all you can think of is that one stupid song and all other options go out the window! Don't do this to your listener! They are working hard to process new information, so don't stifle their response. Your task is to learn something new, not to suggest solutions you've already thought of to the other person. The ability of others to piece your puzzle together will amaze you—but if you're constantly providing answers to them, you won't learn anything new. So, after you complete your elevator pitch, sit down, shut up, and *listen.*

Talk less than the other person. Ask a ton of questions. Pay attention to answers that challenge your thinking or sound like ideal solutions. If you're asked questions, which you will be, answer honestly about what you do and don't know. Keep your commitments in mind to stay true to all the hard work you've already done. Bring the notes you've made throughout this process with you! Be a sponge and you'll get everything you need and more out of these conversations. Every meeting will go differently, and that's a good thing. You might go into one conversation looking for an introduction only to receive a job offer or another surprising opportunity instead. That's awesome! If you go in with one goal but receive something else, you've still succeeded! Go in with good intentions and be open to wherever that conversation might lead.

Avoid the used-car-salesman approach to networking by staying true to you and being vulnerable. **Authenticity in networking is everything.**

Last but not least in the networking conversation strategy is the follow-up. News flash: you are not the only person poking around the job market. If you're networking with an old boss or a friendly coworker, they are likely having similar conversations with other people just like you. Additionally, your networking partners are busy! You need to do anything you can to stand out and stay top of mind. Thankfully, there is a simple, cost-effective way to stand out from the crowd: the old-school, handwritten thank-you note.

I've seen handwritten notes make the difference between yes or no in a sales pitch, the thing that solidifies a professional relationship, or the X factor that moves someone on to the second round of interviews. Don't be too cool or too busy for this step. Buy some stationery, grab your favorite pen, and write a sincere thank-you to every person you have a networking meeting with, regardless of how much their time or energy helped you. Not only will this make you look insanely awesome to your network (does no one write letters anymore?), but it will also encourage people to advocate on your behalf, even when you're not around. The handwritten note is a dying art and it will make you stand out from the crowd.

Avoid the Common Networking Pitfalls

Networking has definite pitfalls that you'll want to avoid, the first being not to request help in the first place. Don't be the person who's too proud or too cool to ask for help. Seriously. You're better than that.

The second mistake people make is ending a conversation without a plan. My golden rule of networking is to never leave a meeting without another meeting. By that, I mean make sure you leave every networking conversation with some sort of follow-up on the books: an introduction they committed to, a lunch meeting they want to set up with you and someone else, another meeting after they think about what you've presented to them. Your job is to make sure that something proactive and future focused comes out of the meeting. Remember the kiss of death is the dreaded "I'll keep you in mind" response. Don't settle for that! This is your opportunity to get what you need, so don't let it go without a fight.

I can't emphasize this enough. I've had clients who've been really excited about tapping their network only to hit repeated dead ends. They tell me that no one in their network can help them, nobody knows anyone. Worst of all, they accept the dreaded "I'll keep you in mind" response. The best way to avoid this all-too-easy pitfall is to schedule a follow-up with each person you meet with for a few weeks down the road. This can be as simple as touching base via email or as personal as a conversation over coffee. You never know what new information people may have or what new people they might have met.

The third mistake is not identifying and/or creating career advocates. Advocates are the key to your success. Remember not everyone in your network will reach the status of advocate. That's okay! At least a handful of the people you talk to want to do more for you . . . so let them! Whether that means writing you a recommendation, editing your résumé, or putting you up for a potential role, if someone offers you extra effort, take it. But you need to form relationships that extend beyond the moment. Each of your career advocates should be ready and feel comfortable to campaign for you when you need them. If you're not creating and leveraging relationships as deep as this, then you're missing the point of networking. Get so excited about your future career that people can't help but want to advocate on your behalf.

The fourth mistake is settling for weak advice. This idea might give you pause, but stick with me here. Especially at the beginning, you might settle for someone's well-meaning but ultimately crappy advice. For years (years!), every time I called up my loving family and told them how miserable I was, I received the same canned advice:

"You should be happy to have that job."
"You can't leave a job without another job."
"Keep working hard and maybe it will get better."

At the time, I was thankful for their positivity, but looking back, I wish I had pushed a little harder or started looking for advice elsewhere sooner. Most people give the advice that they would likely take. If someone tells you that you can't quit a job that makes you miserable, it's probably because *they* would be afraid to quit their own job in that scenario. If someone tells you that your dream job doesn't exist, it's likely because *they* haven't heard of it before. Don't settle for this advice. Look for people who will challenge your thinking and push you to the edge of your comfort zone. That's where the magic happens.

Networking is both a short-term and long-term strategy. In the short term, you're looking for advice, counsel, introductions, and opportunities. That should be pretty clear by now. The long-term strategy is building lifelong advocates. People who will say, "I knew her when" or "I got to see her life transform right before my eyes." Build long-lasting relationships with people who've seen you at your most vulnerable and helped you turn your life around. Not every person in your growing network will fall into this category, but the glorious few who do will be with you on this train of life for the entire thrilling ride.

BECOME UNSTOPPABLE:
STELLAR NETWORKING STRATEGIES

Step 1: Start with who you know.

Remember how to eat an elephant? One bite at a time. The same can be said for networking. Begin with one meeting, and work your way up from there. I recommend identifying the three to five most highly leveraged relationships in your current network to start with. Reach out to each person with your pitch (an email or call is fine) in order to set up meetings. People are busy, so remember that following up will be the name of the game!

Step 2: Define your first set of career advocates.

Does anyone stand out in this audit? Someone who's well connected, extremely positive, and exists within a diverse network? Perhaps it's the person who's been pushing you to pursue work you love all along. Only you can select your advocates and then ignite them to become your biggest fans. Do not underestimate the value of these people! Identify three to five people who you would consider to be your best advocates, and then get ready to have productive networking conversations in the next few steps.

Step 3: Prepare for the conversation.

In advance, work out what you hope to gain from the meeting and prepare an opening statement that will ingratiate you and explain your agenda. Each conversation should have its own purpose, even if it's largely the same. Use that purpose to rehearse your pitch and prepare questions so that you feel ready.

Step 4: Approaching the meeting.

Having done all your homework, you can go into your meeting ready to put your best foot forward. Follow the process laid out in this chapter, but don't stress too much if the conversation takes a few twists and turns. You're not a robot, after all. Here's a general flow to know you're on the right track:

Say "thank you."
Rearticulate your purpose for meeting.
Share your pitch (enroll, envision, ask).
Ask and answer questions.
Listen for answers. (Take notes!)

Step 5: Settle on an actionable, scheduled next step.

Don't leave that meeting without a next step! Don't do it! You'll thank me later.

Step 6: Write and send a thank-you note.

Never underestimate the power of a good old-fashioned thank-you card received by mail. I even have personal stationery and a wax seal with my initial. Yes, that's a bit much—but I'm a bit much sometimes.

Step 7: Begin growing your network.

Keep working this process to learn more about your niche and how to realize it. Practice the A.B.C.s of networking laid out in this chapter and avoid the pitfalls as you do. As you become more experienced in networking, you'll find that asking for introductions to specific people is the best way to expand your network strategically. If you find your networking stalls, review the networking pitfalls and troubleshoot. Don't give in to defeat! One conversation may fizzle, but that doesn't mean there's no one out there who can and wants to help you succeed.

"Man, alone, has the power to transform his thoughts into physical reality; man, alone, can dream and make his dreams come true."

NAPOLEON HILL

LITTLE BETS LEAD
TO BIG WINS

NOW THAT WE'VE covered an extensive amount of information about the value of your network and how to tap it effectively, we can move on to the next step in the Drive phase of the Nth Degree: Navigate. Networking is powerful, but conversations can only get you so far. Tapping into the power of people will help you explore faster and uncover hidden opportunities. What it can't do is determine or decide if those opportunities are the right ones for you. For that, we will lean on a few specific strategies that fall under the heading of Navigate.

We live in a world of constant information overwhelm. It's no wonder that FOMO—fear of missing out—has become so pervasive. At any given moment, you could doing one of thousands of amazing activities and we now have multiple social media channels (Instagram, Facebook, Snapchat, Twitter, LinkedIn, etc.) to show you what you've missed. With all the opportunities to see everyone doing everything imaginable, we often struggle to find life fulfilling and our social calendars always seem like they could be fuller.

If it doesn't feel like this already, your career search will eventually provoke a similar feeling of overwhelm. Even with your niche narrowly defined, there are so many career options to choose from. At this point, I like to think of your niche like the trunk of a tree—it's the big picture version of your vision. The branches of the tree represent the core viable options that fit within this vision. The individual twigs on each branch of the tree represent specific companies or organizations within that option. The leaves on each of these twigs represent specific openings or job opportunities to which you could apply. By now, you've likely identified the trunk of your tree along with some of its branches. However, there are still an unknowable number of twigs and leaves yet to be discovered... You have only one life and a finite amount of time in which to make decisions. This can quickly make career navigation scary and overwhelming. That was my experience until I got a valuable lesson to reframe my career decisions into little bets.

Little Bets for Big Career Wins

Little Bets, by Peter Sims, is a book about finding small ways to explore and develop larger ideas. It was written for practitioners of design thinking who need to rapidly ideate, prototype, and iterate ideas for products. Sims describes each little bet as a low-risk activity—a minimum viable possibility—that furthers a larger idea.[10] Instead of going all in on a project before you know if it works, you can use little bets to prove the viability of the eventual product. While Sims focuses mainly on using this approach to develop products and build companies, I think the little bets approach applies equally well to our task: career navigation. In the same way that Chris Rock tests his comedy material on small audiences or Jeff Bezos uses tiny markets to try new products and services for Amazon, you can make teeny-tiny bets to inform your most important idea—your future.

Little bets allow you to quickly test out a large amount of small ideas without too much of a downside in the case that you're wrong. This strategy avoids putting too much pressure on any one idea. That way, if you do fail, you'll do so quickly and without massive repercussions. In your career, this could be akin to taking a night class before deciding to invest in a master's degree. Little bets are minimum viable ways to learn more about what fits you. Instead of focusing on the gaps in your résumé or what other people will think of you or the word "failure," concentrate your efforts on making tiny bets to invest in your career, to get to your ideal future state faster. If you don't want to waste weeks, months, or years trying to figure out the exact right track, then this approach is for you. If you feel stuck or rigid or afraid of making the wrong decision, little bets allow you to tinker, tweak, and even be playful in the discovery of your future career. Leverage this proven creative process and you'll end up innovating your life.

Six Little Bets for Your Career Happiness

When it comes to career MVPs (minimum viable possibilities), I have six top recommendations for making little bets on your future career.

The simplest and tiniest of these is none other than *conducting your own online research*. Now, I know that earlier I told you to avoid Google and Indeed, but at this point, you're ready. With your niche, you're armed with the information you need to use the internet effectively. Want to learn how to hotwire a car? There's a YouTube video for that. Want to try your hand at screenwriting? There's a MasterClass for that. Want to know what it would be like to be an Alaskan fisherman? There's a specific meet-up group for that. Doing some minimal research into your field, along with applying what you're learning from strategic networking, can open up worlds of opportunities. You could discover entire branches that fit well into your career tree you may never have heard of before! Learning about your field of interest online is the smallest bet you can make on your future career happiness. Do not apply for or take a job without having done at least this minimal amount of research.

The next little bet on your career is *taking a class* in that field or industry. Entire companies are dedicated to giving individuals the skills and knowledge they need to excel at whatever career they see fit. General Assembly, for example, offers expert-led training in data, design, digital marketing, and more. Udemy and Coursera offer both free and paid online education in just about everything. Local universities offer night and weekend classes if you're considering the need for more traditional school. Instead of going all in and enrolling in school for years only to discover that you don't need that degree to get the job you want, try out small opportunities to increase your learning. I was considering going back to school, but first I took a General Assembly class called How to Start a Business in Thirty Days. Turns out, I didn't need that MBA after all. You may discover a passion for a subject you didn't expect or you may realize that going back to school is not for you and thus dodge a long and expensive bullet.

The third little bet you can make is *doing informational interviews*. This is my personal favorite, because I'm a people person. The concept is simple: find someone whose career you think you might like, want, or otherwise admire, sit down with them, and ask them about it. People love talking about themselves, so this little bet is among the easier ones to put into action. After I completed Semester at Sea, I did nothing but informational interviews. I went to Google and interviewed someone in people analytics. I went to Facebook to talk to someone in human resources. I traveled the country asking others about what they did and why. Informational interviews will give you a deeper understanding of industries, an inside view of a particular role or company, and intel about whether you could work with people like the ones you interview.

The fourth tiny career bet is one that, for some reason, we've forgotten all about: *shadowing*. Shadowing is the lost art of spending some time in an environment to make sure it's a good fit. We so readily dive into the deep end with internships and full-time jobs, but whatever happened to the simple take-your-kid-to-work-day approach to career development? Job shadowing is basic, but the insights gained from it are invaluable. By following someone around, watching their activities, seeing who they interact with, and noting their necessary knowledge and expertise, you can either discover your life's work or scratch something off the list. I discovered this lesson when I was just seven years old. My mom brought me to her office for a day, and within the first fifteen minutes of watching her sit at her desk and type, I proudly proclaimed that I hated it and would never work at an office job. Only later in life did I put this lesson into practice, and I haven't worked at a desk job since. Shadowing is a little bet that is too valuable not to leverage.

The fifth little bet on my list is the least popular but one of the most effective: *volunteering*. Like you, I don't enjoy giving my precious time away for nothing. But when you're learning as you work for free, you're getting massive value in exchange. You're gathering lessons about what you like to do (or don't!). As Mark Manson says, and pardon my language, every job has a shit sandwich that will be thrown

With clarity of purpose
and conviction of vision,
**you will never worry
about making the wrong
decision or missing out
on something better.**

at you some point.[11] If you can figure out what that is and whether it's something you can deal with, then you've learned something useful. I have a good friend who's now the CEO of a company, but do you know how he got started? Volunteering. He spent his nights and weekends moonlighting for this company and slowly worked his way up to employee, then management, then CEO. Done right, working without pay is not without reward. It's another little bet on your career happiness.

The last little bet on your future career is an iteration of the previous one. Instead of working for free, *try freelancing*. I was a freelance writer long before I started blogging for myself and my own business. I've written everything from content for an online psychology textbook to career quizzes to buyer's guides. You can learn so much from freelancing. It teaches you whether what you want to do has value in the marketplace—in other words, will anyone pay you for it? It proves to you whether the activity is something you could do full-time or if it's just a means to an end. Lastly, it shows you whether you have the stomach for entrepreneurship or sales. Freelancing could be your first step into a future business or the confirmation you need to stay in a more stable career. Either way, trying your hand at it is a little bet to learn a big lesson.

The Ultimate Benefit of Tiny Bets

A little career bet can help you avoid making colossal career mistakes. I've shared my favorite tiny career bets, but the variety of little bets is limited only by your creativity. When planning your little bets, think about your end goal and viable ways you could test out that idea. Want to write a book? Start with a blog. Want to start a company? Begin by selling your product or service to one client.

A word of warning: tiny bets may not completely alleviate your career FOMO. I still wonder if I should take time off to go to business school or if I can carve out a few months to travel and simultaneously grow my business. From time to time, I still think about what I might be missing out on. The main difference is that now I question with hope, not fear. I used to be desperate—living in a constant state of FOMO because I hated my job and would have given my left arm to do anything else. Having gone through the same career clarity process you are working on now, I can tell you that I live with more purpose and intention. I actively choose the projects and programs I work on, and the partners I work with, just as you are about to do. When you build a career with this serious intentionality, you'll know that you've made decisions in service of a greater good. I might never go to business school, but I do pursue my passions, follow my dream to bring people to life at work, run a company that aligns with my vision, and change lives along the way. Right now, that's good enough for me to feel good about my decisions.

When you achieve clarity about your career, the opportunities that used to look shiny and tempting will pale in comparison to your life and the purpose you're pursuing. I recommend that you pursue each individual path—the branches, twigs, and leaves of your tree—to test and gain certainty along the way. Use little bets along with the networking tactics you've been practicing to gather more information. As you follow each viable path, the right opportunities will present themselves at the right time and you'll be there to seize them. Best of all, because you're nurturing more than one branch of the tree, if you ever hit a dead end, you'll have other options at the ready. You'll never be stuck again.

BECOME UNSTOPPABLE:
YOUR BEST LITTLE BETS

Step 1: Brainstorm using the six little bets.

Relating to your niche and everything you've learned from networking, brainstorm six little bets, one for each of the areas we discussed in this chapter:

1 Researching online
2 Taking a course
3 Informational interviewing
4 Shadowing
5 Volunteering
6 Freelancing

Step 2: Brainstorm alternative little bets you could make on your career.

Remember that little bets are limited only by your imagination. Do at least the bare minimum to see if you'll truly like the niche you're pursuing. Inspect what you expect from any given situation.

Step 3: Place at least one little bet.

Ask yourself which bets are best to test any remaining assumptions or questions you have about that career. Worried about what the environment will be like? Test it. Worried about the people you'll be working with? Test it. Worried about making an all-in bet only to be even more miserable than you already are? Test it. Review your list of bets and execute at least one.

"Inaction breeds doubt and
fear. Action breeds confidence
and courage. If you want to conquer
fear, do not sit at home and think
about it. Go out and get busy."

DALE CARNEGIE

CREATE A NINETY-DAY
ACTION PLAN

ASSIM NICHOLAS TALEB, a scholar who focuses on statistics and randomness and whose book *The Black Swan* is said to be one of the most influential pieces of literature since World War II, wrote, "Life is about execution rather than purpose."[12] When I first read that quote, I scoffed. While I was researching this book and the Nth Degree's programs and courses, I contemplated purpose a lot about more than I did execution. "Purposeful intention is really where the rubber meets the road," I thought. Taleb's quote seemed to fly in the face of my "purpose is everything" theory. And unfortunately, like all practical but annoying advice, it's correct.

You can have all the purpose in the world, but without action, who really cares? Without action, how will your purpose be fulfilled? Without action, how will anything, including your career, change?

Action is the not-so-secret key to accomplishment. Given the connectivity of our world, the readily available amounts of information on the internet, the deteriorating formalities of society, the barriers to entry in almost every field, and the pervasiveness of impressive résumés, there's no difference between what you and anyone else have the potential to accomplish. The person who takes the most frequent, consistent, and right actions will win. This is why it's crucial to cultivate a willingness to act. Do, fail, recover, repeat, and succeed. Your willingness to be wrong to eventually be right. To get back up and keep trying. In short, to act.

Not *Any* Action, Right Action

If action is essential, you might think that the busiest person will eventually win the day. However, any one of us who's spent time on activities that have proved fruitless will tell you that it's not just about action—it's about *right* action. So, what stands between you and decisive, necessary, right action? Paralysis by analysis.

If I had a dime for every time I heard one of these excuses, I'd be a very rich woman:

"I don't know where to start."
"I tried, and it's just not possible."
"I just need some help."
"If only I had more resources/money/time/help."
"Someone's already doing it."
"I'm trapped/stuck/confused/overwhelmed/tired/scared..."
"I don't have enough information."
"It's not the right time."

You get the idea.

I'd argue that all these excuses can be boiled down to the one real problem that's at the root of our inaction, insecurities, and inability to choose. That problem? Fear. Fear is the number-one thing that stands in the way of action. Its impact keeps us from moving forward. Keeps us from our dreams. And, more importantly, keeps us from *right* action.

Right actions move the needle in service of the whole. They are the key indicators of your success. Right actions propel you forward rather than keeping you active yet ultimately running in place. There's a big difference between scrolling a job board for an hour and having an hour-long, dedicated career networking conversation. One *feels* productive while the other creates real traction. The real reason we rely on fruitless activities or choose no activity at all is usually the lack of an action plan. Imagine looking at a to-do list that starts with "find your dream job" and looking at one that breaks down the teeny-tiny steps it takes to get there. One is overwhelming and causes paralysis. The other is bite-sized and encourages activity. When your to-do list consists of "send email" and "schedule networking meeting," it's not so daunting. It's precisely those tiny but not-so-trivial actions that are necessary to achieve your goal and turn your vision into your reality.

If you're unconvinced, think about this: how different do you feel now than when you started this process? Do you remember when you used to say you'd never find work you loved or you felt completely and irreversibly stuck? Look at you now! You're networking your butt off and navigating down the path of your own unique vision for success. You're a career rock star in the making, and all it took was breaking down the process into simple, digestible steps to go from stuck to unstoppable. (If you feel like you've just been worked over by a Jedi, don't worry. That's how you're supposed to feel.)

Your Unique Action Plan

Your next task is to break down the milestones, tactics, and actions that you'll need to succeed. As the title of this chapter suggests, I recommend starting with a ninety-day action plan. There are, of course, some extenuating circumstances that could either shorten this plan or prolong it. No two job searches are identical in length. For instance, if you're currently unemployed, then you'll likely have more time each day to dedicate to the search process, so perhaps your timeline could shrink to sixty or even thirty days. For others, if you've identified an unalterable need for more schooling or certifications (which is rare but sometimes unavoidable), then your timeline will be longer. Could you land your dream job in nine days or ninety days or (God forbid) 900 days? Yes. But ninety days is a reasonable, realistic amount of time with which to begin the planning process.

A word of caution for you uber-planner people. Creating a plan is a form of action, but *over*-planning and *perfecting* without actually doing anything to move the needle is yet another form of avoidance and inaction. As Og Mandino wisely wrote in the book *The Greatest Salesman in the World*:

> Never has there been a map, however carefully executed to detail and scale, which carried its owner over even one inch of ground. Never has there been a parchment of law, however fair, which prevented one crime. Never has there been a scroll, even such as the one I hold, which earned so much as a penny or produced a single word of acclamation. Action, alone, is the tinder which ignites the map, the parchment, this scroll, my dreams, my plans, my goals, into a living force. Action is the food and drink which will nourish my success.
>
> I will act now.[13]

Make the plan. Work the plan. Adapt the plan. Act.

Action Plans for Non-Planners

Not being a naturally gifted planner myself, I lean on the expertise of others. Recently, I discovered the real value of Stephen Covey's idea of setting rocks within a larger plan to achieve a goal. The term "rocks" comes from a famous analogy that Covey used in his book *First Things First*. He demonstrated that if you want to fill a jar with sand, pebbles, and rocks, the best way to make sure everything fits is to put the rocks in first. In fact, the only way to make sure that the rocks will fit *at all* is to put them in first. If, instead, you fill your jar with sand and pebbles first, which represent the meaningless everyday activities that make you *feel* productive, then you won't have any room for the important stuff—the rocks.[14] Use this wisdom to your advantage. What major goals or milestones will you need accomplish on the way to your career success? Perhaps you need to further define your niche into a viable set of job titles. Maybe you need to identify all of the branches of your tree to make sure you've covered all your options. If you begin with these larger goals or milestones in your search—your rocks—then the smaller daily activities will serve to move you toward these goals.

The simple key to your no-fail action plan is to discern which tactics will move the needle in the direction of a career you love. This will require you looking back at everything you've gathered so far to figure out which search activities are working best for you. Are you a natural and savvy networker who will benefit most from having more valuable networking conversations? Are you a creative and fast worker who will gain from more free work opportunities to test out your skills? Are you a gifted interviewer who will win by continuing to ask solid questions to new and different people in informational interviews? Identify your top indicators of success,

Make the plan.
Work the plan.
Adapt the plan.
Act.

and commit to doing those things in a well-defined routine. Remember to make the plan, work the plan, and adapt the plan, as needed.

The smaller you can make the actions within the plan, the better. Yes, honor the rocks, but in order to really tackle them, break them down into manageable tasks. Imagine the difference between committing to losing twenty pounds or to doing ten push-ups per day. The thought of everything it will take to lose the weight sounds daunting, so we put it off. But the thought of doing just ten push-ups per day? Easy! And the best part is that once you drop down to do your ten push-ups, you're already on the floor, so it's that much easier to crank out one or two more if the spirit moves you. If not, simply celebrate that you met your tiny, surmountable goal. Yet another Jedi mind trick.

At this stage of the process, you're going to be doing a lot of scheduling. Pull out your calendar and make some serious (but small!) commitments to yourself. Plan out at least the next ninety days of your career navigation. Start with the big milestones (perhaps job title, strategic conversation with current boss, and interviewing), and work backward. If you want a job offer ninety days from now, ask yourself what needs to happen in three months, two months, and one month. Commit to doing at least one action—yes, just *one* action—each day that will get you closer to your next milestone. By focusing on one effective, right action, you'll avoid overwhelm and indecision. You'll also be able to focus on doing one thing extremely well rather than several things averagely (or worse, doing nothing at all!). With each day, each new win, each time you live up to your own expectations, you're building the muscle necessary to become a person of action.

What's the simple secret to becoming a person of action now and for the rest of your life? As Nike says, just do it!

Take. Decisive. Action. Daily. If, every day for ninety days in a row, you take decisive action that leads you toward your goal, you'll begin to see massive change. Practicing these habits will ultimately form you into a person who chooses action over inaction, learning over ruminating, and creating a life you love over paralyzing indecision.

BECOME UNSTOPPABLE: YOUR UNIQUE ACTION PLAN

Step 1: Assess where you are now.

Consider all your opportunities for career networking and navigation: online research, informational interviews, shadowing, freelancing, volunteering, strategic networking, and any others that come to mind.

Look at your current progress objectively. What do you really need to move the needle forward? An introduction to someone specific? A job title or role description? A contact in a new industry? A business plan? Whatever you need, get crystal clear on it as this will help define the best first steps of your action plan.

Step 2: Grab a ninety-day calendar and get planning.

Start with the big milestones for one, two, and three months. Then work backward. Determine a small and tangible action to do each day that is (a) based on your assessment of where you're at now, (b) easy enough to execute on a given day, and (c) a step closer to your goal. This is an opportunity to build a foundation of simple tasks in order to avoid overwhelm by focusing on the micro-actions that will add up to major change.

Step 3: Run your action plan by a friend or mentor.

Ask this person to poke holes in it or explain your action plan back to you. It should be logical and functional. Remember: right action, not any action.

Step 4: Get started!

Action is everything. With each tiny action item you complete, you will learn something new. And with each new bit of information, you'll be able to move faster and more efficiently to your ideal career.

"If you have felt hopelessness, hold on! Wonderful changes are going to happen in your life as you begin to live it on purpose."

RICK WARREN

CONQUER DESPAIR,
DOUBT, AND DEFEAT

I F YOU'VE DISCOVERED your true value through the exercises of Now, Nature, and Nurture; pieced those insights together to define your unique genius zone with the Niche exercises; and embraced the strategies in Drive to create your unique action plan using the tools outlined in Network and Navigate, then you are *living* the Nth Degree. You are now on *the* proven path to living and working in your ideal career. You are doing everything you need to do to become unstoppable.

Please acknowledge that this is no small accomplishment. You have done work that most people will never have the courage to even consider doing in their lifetime. You've challenged your own limiting beliefs. You've unburdened yourself of the unnecessary expectations of others. You've looked despair, doubt, and defeat in the face and chosen courage instead. Now we want to ensure we capture that progress and avoid the temptation to fall back into old ways of thinking.

The final step of the Nth Degree, Nourish, is so important. If you've spent even a day networking and navigating toward your ideal career, then you know that the career search is no simple or linear exercise. The search process can be arduous, cumbersome, demoralizing, and seemingly indefinite. Even after you've braved the search and landed in your next (and ideal) gig, you'll have to contend with the inevitable change that life throws your way. Nourish represents the process by which you prepare yourself for the journey ahead. Together, we will identify your support systems, motivation banks, and emotional backstops to help you keep going when the going gets tough.

Living your life with the Nth Degree in mind means committing to consistent reevaluation and career evolution. The journey from hating your job to *loving* your life lasts, well, a lifetime. I'm sure that's not what you want to hear, but it's the true nature of life. As one of my business coaches says, when you begin a journey, you start as You, Version 1 with Goal, Version 1. Then as you progress toward that goal, you evolve into You, Version 2 who will, of course, have an updated Goal, Version 2. If we do this right, then we are constantly cycling upward, becoming and pursuing even better versions of ourselves. You know all too well by now that the only constant in life is change. To thrive within that reality, I encourage you to create mechanisms that nourish and encourage the best version of you to keep going. Keep progressing. Keep learning. Keep trying.

Your Reason for Being

One of the best cases I can make for your continued effort is that it will lead to continued learning. Every day I move forward in my business with the best of intentions, knowing that I'll inevitably learn better or learn something new. Just recently, thinking I had my whole career coaching approach figured out, I was gifted with a new lesson which updated my thinking. One of my clients shared a centuries-old Japanese concept that perfectly sums up the pursuit of a long and happy career better than I ever could: it's called ikigai.

The word "ikigai" roughly translates to "reason for being," much like the French phrase "raison d'être." Ikigai is a combination of two Japanese root words: "iki," meaning life, and "gai," meaning value or worth. In Japanese culture, everyone on this planet has an ikigai. To find it, we have to search deep within ourselves and our surroundings to uncover what brings us meaning and satisfaction. Your ikigai is your source life's value. It's what makes the days, weeks, months, and years of your life worthwhile. Living your ikigai is also what makes *you feel* the most valuable. Using this concept as a model, ikigai looks much like your Niche. True ikigai is where four core components of your career meet: (1) what you love, (2) what you're good at, (3) what the world needs, and (4) what you can get paid for. Knowing your ikigai is the greatest litmus test of whether you're living your career to your fullest potential. Defining it is the core exercise of Nourish because this ikigai is foundational to your ideal career pursuit.

At any given time, you can fall into one of a handful of less-than-ideal places in the ikigai model. This happens when you're missing any one (or more) of the four essential components. While my first job felt like a complete mismatch, it turns out I was only missing two ikigai core concepts. Surprisingly, I had two major components of the ikigai concept in place. I got paid and the world needed it. I was definitely missing the other two components because I wasn't particularly gifted at finance and I definitely didn't love it. Even as I got better at my job, I lacked true love and passion for it, so at best I could be comfortable, but I would always have a feeling of emptiness that needed to be satisfied somewhere else. Perhaps you've had, or even have right now, a job that makes

Knowing your ikigai
is the greatest litmus test
of whether you're living
your career to your fullest
potential.

you feel like this. You go through the motions, getting paid, doing something that the world needs, that you may happen to be decent at doing, but you don't love it and it will never be more than a job for you. A profession but not your calling. Not your reason for being. Not your ikigai.

To begin testing for your ikigai, evaluate where you are right now. If you have any two components of ikigai, then you have a passion, a mission, a vocation, or a profession. If you have three, then we're getting a little closer. There are so many ways to get this *almost* right. But when you have all four of these components, you're never going to look back. And if you do, you'll see all the hard work you've done as completely worthwhile. While you're still conducting your search, ikigai is a good way to think about your vision and strengthen your commitment to creating that reality. Once you've landed in a new position, you can ask yourself periodically if it continues to fulfill all four aspects of ikigai. If you want to pivot in your work, add a new product to your offerings, hire someone, change roles, negotiate salary, or otherwise make a professional move, use ikigai as a barometer for the best choice for you.

Once you've had a few networking conversations and you've really started to navigate down your handful of viable paths, you'll begin to consider job offers, industry opportunities, and more possibilities than you can even imagine. If you keep your commitments at your side and ikigai as your true north, you can't go wrong. Yes, you might feel overwhelmed, confused, or scared of making the wrong decision at times. But with these tools in your toolkit, you'll stay on the path to the work of your dreams.

Creating Your Personal Motivation Bank

If ikigai serves as your light at the end of the tunnel, then you'll still need a flashlight to illuminate your way until you get there. You've done some amazing work, some hard work, some work that probably felt impossible before you got started. Somewhere along the way, you might have come close to quitting. We're never free from the voices that say, "This isn't going to work for me" or "I've tried this already and nothing changed."

At this point in the program, it's important to learn what got you through this process. Ask yourself a few critical questions:

What has kept you going?
Why haven't you quit?
Where does that motivation come from?

My guess is that you have discovered a meaning deeper than a new title, bigger paycheck, or more vacation days. If that was all you wanted, then you likely wouldn't be reading this book. So, if you had to name it, what motivates you? If you can get clear on that—if you can identify the why behind what you're doing—then nothing can stop you. Use your specific, unique reason for choosing this pursuit—for aiming at extraordinary rather than ordinary—to find the courage to keep going.

While I was on Semester at Sea, I heard the best example of this type of motivation bank. I was working with a professor who specialized in design thinking. He had staked his entire professional career on the idea that we are all inherently creative and that by tapping into this creativity, we can change the world for the better. One day I sat down with him and asked if we could dive deep; I was still confused about the prospects for my career and wondered if I would ever find something I cared about so much that I wouldn't get bored or burned out. That was a pattern that I was aching to break. He shared his real reason for investing in and nurturing creativity. It turns out that he was Christian and believed in a higher power who was the ultimate creator of the universe. In Christian beliefs, human beings are said to be created in the image and likeness of God. To my professor, it stood to reason that if God is the ultimate creator and we are made in his likeness, then we are all endowed with inherent and limitless creativity. He believed that if he could nurture and uncover the creativity in even one person, he was participating in something divine. He was making the world a better and more spiritual place every single day.

I walked away from that conversation with my jaw on the ground. To think that someone had drawn a direct line from spirituality to creativity to human beings to work and finally to design thinking was more than I could comprehend at the time. And perhaps you're feeling the same way. If all you've ever known about work is that it's hard, a slog, a nine-to-five, a paycheck, or otherwise a barely tolerable experience, then this idea will sound foreign if not completely outrageous. But if you really leaned into the Nth Degree, then you probably have a similar motivation for your ideal career. It's more than a job to you. This meaning doesn't necessarily have to be spiritual in nature. It doesn't even have to make sense to anyone else! All that deeper meaning has to do is motivate *you*.

For me, that deeper why is this: I believe that we are *alive* for a reason. I believe that we are all *unique* for a reason. And I believe that if I can help someone put these two ideas together—how they are unique and why they are here—then I can help someone fulfill their personal destiny and unleash their true potential in the world. For a small moment in a small space in time, my efforts have ripple effects that go on to make this world a better place because one more person is living and working in their genius zone. That is my ultimate motivation.

So, what is it for you? What's kept you going this far? And what will keep you going as you continue to navigate through your unique set of opportunities to find your unique niche and career? Define it and set it as a reminder of the future you are traveling toward.

Looking for a career you love will never be easy. But the people who are successful in this pursuit have a deeper purpose and intention to their search that mobilizes them and others in a way that no salary, benefit, or title ever could. For you to thrive in your pursuit and eventually land upon your goal, given all of the ups and downs in the process, you need a clear purpose to drive all that you do.

Slaying Your Inner Dragon

No matter how hard you work, no matter how aligned you are, and no matter how motivated you may be, there will always be one hurdle, one barrier, one dragon that will appear along your journey. We've talked about it before: fear.

Every choice in life is dictated by love or fear. I learned this from Marianne Williamson, who's famous for her connection to *A Course in Miracles*, her bestselling book *A Return to Love*, and her spiritual teaching, which has been quoted by Nelson Mandela. In *A Return to Love*, Williamson writes that love is to fear as light is to darkness. Just as darkness is really only the absence of light, fear is really only the absence of love.[15] So, when the mind is filled with love—abundance, joy, hope, and possibility—there cannot be fear, just as when a room is full of light, there cannot be darkness.

While that might sound pretty woo-woo for a book on career-building, consider this: what's the number one thing holding you back from taking a leap into a career you love? Why do we even call it a leap in the first place? It's scary! It takes courage! You feel like you're moving from something known to something unknown, which is inherently unsafe. Even Elizabeth Gilbert, most famous for her bestselling book *Eat Pray Love*, writes in *Big Magic* that "the real reason we don't move creatively ahead is always and only fear."[16]

You name it, we're afraid of it. Fear keeps us in crappy jobs, sucky relationships, and less-than-fulfilling friendships. Just as we need to own the reality that life is going to constantly change, we need to embrace this truth as well: *fear is never going away.* That's because fear has an important biological function. Fear has the biological and historical purpose of keeping us *alive.* Without it, we'd all be up for a Darwin Award for stupidest death. The important thing to remember, as Gilbert writes, is that times have changed. Instead of venturing into the deep dark woods, you're just trying to write a poem, tell someone "I love you," or maybe find a job that makes you happy. Because of this fact, we can begin to understand and treat our fear differently. You don't have to give your fear total control. As Gilbert writes, fear doesn't need to be in the driver's seat: let it ride in the back with the luggage, far away from the radio dial and, most importantly, the navigation system. Imagine thinking of fear in that way. You might see that you take some of its power away.

A beautiful and famous sentiment is that courage is not the absence of fear, only the decision that something else is more important. The moment I heard that, I decided to find something—anything—that was more important than fear. For me, that something was living a life that I believed in, one with no regrets. It was ultimately being able to say that I would not fall victim to what Bronnie Ware says is the number-one regret of the dying: "I wish I had the courage to live a life true to myself, not the life others expected of me."[17] In order to keep all your gains, your job now is to bring your fears to the surface, be open and honest about them, and surrender them (knowing they aren't going anywhere). You must also decide what, in this lifetime, is more important to you than holding on to your fear. This will help you transform into something even greater and give you the final bit of nourishment you need to take your career to the Nth Degree.

BECOME UNSTOPPABLE:
YOUR SOURCES OF NOURISHMENT

Step 1: Identify your ikigai.
Remember your ikigai has four distinct components:

1 What you love
2 What you're good at
3 What the world needs
4 What you can get paid for

Think objectively about where you are in your career right now. Does it meet all four of these requirements for a reason for being? If you're reading this book, the likely answer is no. Record your insights about what exactly is missing. Next, look at the niche you've crafted. Does it meet all four requirements? If you're following along with the exercises in this book, the answer will be yes. If the answer is no, then ask yourself what needs to be added to fulfill this concept. Any time you're considering a significant change in your career, pull out this model to reassess whether all four points will be covered in your next move.

Step 2: Create a conceptual motivation bank.

Define your why so that you have a reminder when the going gets tough. Begin by answering these questions:

What has kept you going thus far?
Why haven't you quit?
Where does your motivation come from?
What matters more to you than an impressive title, bigger paycheck, or more vacation days?
If you had to put a name on it, what's your why?

Take these questions deeper by considering the connection between what you believe and the work you want to do. If you can link what you believe in (for example, human creativity) to what you want to do (for example, teaching design thinking), then you'll have an even deeper motivation to keep going. Reread the professor's and my examples, if needed.

Step 3: Create a tangible motivation bank.

This will be made up of tangible reminders of the purpose behind your pursuit. While I was on Semester at Sea, I created one of these by accident. Every time I saw an inspiring quote, a funny image, a picture of my dream life, a moving conversation with a friend, I made a note of it. I saved them in their various file formats in a folder on my computer called "Happiness Love Joy." Yes, I'm a nerd. Any time I was feeling down, defeated, or desperate for my next gig, I opened that folder and reminded myself of all the incredible motivation and support I had in life. Whether you do this physically or digitally, a motivation bank will serve you when you're experiencing the inevitable doubts along the road to your ideal career.

Step 4: Put fear in the passenger seat.

First of all, you must acknowledge your fear. Here are some of the fears I hear the most:

What if the grass isn't greener?
What if this is the best I can do?
What if my dream job doesn't exist?
What if I fail?
What if this is just a phase, and I get bored when I get there?
What if the unknown is worse than this?
What if I have to start over from scratch?

All of these fears are valid. You and I cannot overcome what we do not acknowledge. So first, be honest with yourself. One of my biggest fears is that I'm not the best and most-equipped steward for my own business. If I kept that to myself, then the burden of solving that problem or overcoming that fear would be all on me. But if I own it and share, then maybe I don't have to be the *only* steward of my business. Maybe I can earn some much-needed help! So what is it that you're really afraid of happening? Write it down.

Second, practice fear-setting. Tim Ferriss gave a great TED Talk called "Why You Should Define Your Fears instead of Your Goals" and I highly encourage you to watch it in full. Basically, he overcomes his fears by not only acknowledging them but taking them to their natural end. He writes down the fear and asks himself, "What are the worst things that would happen if this were true?" Then he brainstorms all the ways he can mitigate or eliminate the potential for these various negative outcomes. If he's afraid that his business will fail without him but he really wants to take a vacation, then he asks himself what could possibly go wrong if he left, and he creates as many plans and systems as possible to keep those things from happening.[18] Practice this and see if it alleviates any short-term fear.

Third, connect with something deeper. What's more important than what you're afraid of happening? Is it no-regrets living? Is it dying knowing you did everything you could to pursue your dream? (Morbid, I know, but nothing motivates like thinking of the end.) Is it being an amazing example for your children? Whatever it is, *connect* with it on a deep, if not spiritual, level. This motivation will be your ultimate foundation for putting fear in the passenger seat and taking control of your own life and career.

CONCLUSION
LIVING TO THE NTH DEGREE

REMEMBER WAY BACK at the beginning of this book when I had my personal awakening moment with Joe? That day, I witnessed what I thought to be a miracle. In a flash, Joe became a new person. He obsessed about engineering and construction. He gushed about bridges and cement and condensation. Then as quickly as it had arrived, that incredible light and energy that had transformed Joe's body and mind was gone. I watched it leave, and I wondered, "Why is someone with true passion and the expertise to live that passion wasting away on a Wall Street trading floor?"

More importantly, why was I??

I had never once *gushed* about high-yield credit. I never once *lit up* about balance sheets. Sadly, I realized I never once *came to life* at my job. And yet, I had been settling for this zombie career that would inevitably lead to me having lived a zombie life (or worse). I reasoned with myself that this was just how work was; I had accepted a job (and a life) that meant nothing to me, did nothing for me except pay my bills, and used none of my gifts or talents or interests. However, on the rooftop that day, I decided no more. Come hell or high water, I was going to find my ideal career and live my life to its fullest degree. Perhaps, right now, that same opportunity is in front of you. The question is: will you choose to take it?

Drawing Your Line in the Sand

Even when your head doesn't know what to do, your heart does. Right now, that little pumper is jockeying with your brain for control of your body. It wants to take over your voice and your physical movements so it can get you out of work you hate and into a job and a life you love! It knows you have an incredible gift to give to the world. It is begging you, in the name of all that is good, not to allow a bad job or a fractured career to erase the memory of who you are—the *best* version of you. Your heart knows you are meaningful. It knows your life has a purpose. It knows that you can and will find it if you choose to look.

As we touched upon in the Nature step, there's a real danger in spending the finite amount of energy you have playing someone else's game in life. My time on Wall Street was the emotional equivalent of being that poor cow in the ocean. Every minute that I spent pretending I liked my job was a minute I could have spent discovering, defining, or driving a career I loved. Every second I spent straining to be someone I wasn't was a second in which I could have successfully (and sustainably) been myself. All the time I spent there scared, I was keeping that spot from someone who would have loved and thrived in that environment.

Don't do this to yourself. Don't let all the work you've done go to waste. There is a career out there which will allow you to be yourself—both successfully *and* sustainably. Until you commit to pursuing it, you'll continue to feel like a person with unrealized potential. Take note from the people around you who are waking up, finding new jobs, performing in those careers, and living great lives. Those people are becoming the next Frank Lloyd Wright while you're still working at an investment bank, writing their first novel while you're filing paperwork, living *their* dream while you're just... well... dreaming about it.

Many people will pick up this book and never put it into action. Don't let that happen to you. Draw your line in the sand now and commit to living as the best and highest version of you.

Learning from the Best

In a 1991 biography by Agnes de Mille, Martha Graham is quoted as having said the following about success and failure:

> There is a vitality, a life force, a quickening that is translated through you into action, and because there is only one of you in all time, this expression is unique. And if you block it, it will never exist through any other medium and be lost. The world will not have it. It is not your business to determine how good it is, nor how valuable it is, nor how it compares with other expressions. It is your business to keep it yours clearly and directly, to keep the channel open. You do not even have to believe in yourself or your work. You have to keep open and aware directly to the urges that motivate you. Keep the channel open.[19]

Ever since I first read this quote, I've kept it near to my heart. In fact, I used it in its entirety in my very first TEDx Talk in 2016.[20] If this quote speaks to you at all, do me this one favor: commit to being the best version of you. Right now.

Stop hiding in bad jobs. Stop pretending to like something because someone told you that's what successful people do. Stop playing someone else's game. Your fate in the endeavor of taking your career from stuck to unstoppable is completely up to you. You get to choose: your passion or someone else's? Your life or someone else's? Your game or someone else's? Redefine success as being the best version of you that you can be—as success that is sustainable because it was made for you. You can only fail if you stop trying or never start. You can only fail by trying to be someone else and hating your life. Don't fail. Don't hate your life.

Still want more proof? Here's the last permission slip you'll ever need.

Your Personal Permission Slip

Right now, you have a lot of tools in your kit. In addition to your Nth Degree strategies, you're now armed with what you need to conquer despair, doubt, and defeat. With your ikigai, your motivation bank, and your fear in the passenger seat, all that's left to take your career from stuck to unstoppable is something you may not realize you need: your permission.

One of my very first clients, Isabel, taught me this valuable lesson. On our fourth of five coaching calls, she finally opened up to me about her resistance to our career-coaching journey. She told me that she had a breakdown the night before one of her networking conversations, because she felt so stuck. She had so many *ideas* about what she wanted to do, but she was trapped in the shoebox of her office. She wanted to be out there, flying, making it happen, but the physical constraints of her environment were so restrictive that she could not see any way out. All the other parts of her day took priority over her dreams. Her biggest worry was that she barely had time to do everything already expected of her. How would she find time to pursue work she actually loved?

During that breakdown, Isabel realized something that changed her world forever and she shared her epiphany with me. Who, if anyone, was going to give her *permission* to make her dreams a *priority*? The answer: no one. No one, but her. Her epiphany was foundational. If you're seeking external permission to prioritize loving your own life, you're going to be looking for a very long time. When she deeply questioned all that she considered to be her priorities and constraints, she realized that she was the bottleneck. She had been waiting for *someone else* to give her permission to put those things aside and spend her energy on something more meaningful, something with purpose. She didn't need or want to abandon all of her responsibilities in life. She simply needed to *prioritize herself* and allow herself to believe before she could move forward and really embrace the idea of living and working in an ideal career. The permission she was waiting for couldn't come from someone else: she needed *permission* from within.

So, in honor of Isabel, I leave all of my clients with this. The last permission slip you will ever need. If necessary, repeat this mantra of permission to yourself:

I give myself permission to pursue my ideal career and life with purpose.

I give myself permission to stop making excuses and start creating the life I really want with intention.

I give myself permission to treat my life and my dreams as a priority, knowing that the best version of me will have greater impact on everyone else.

I give myself permission to find work that I love.

Go out there and be your best self. Navigate your career with purpose. Further your position with positive intent. Store up your motivation for the hard days to come. And remember you don't need anyone else's permission to start your own life. You have your own. And now you can do it.

You Are Unstoppable

Here are my final thoughts on taking your career from stuck to unstoppable. Everything that you do from here on out is up to you. Gone are the days of unconscious living and conscious complaining. You've been enlightened, brought over from the dark side, and you can never go back. Strangely enough, you'll probably go through a short mourning period; I know I did. Although life might not be ideal when you feel stuck and powerless, it becomes comfortable after a while. Once you know your niche, you become infinitely more responsible for your life and career. You've woken up to the reality that you can shape your own destiny. You can't blame others for your unhappiness anymore. You can't use the same old excuses. Now that you're alive, it all comes down to you.

I remember being *freaked* out by that feeling. Not until I was eight chapters in to Chérie Carter-Scott's *If Life Is a Game, These Are the Rules* did my surprisingly negative reaction to taking responsibility start to make sense to me:

> The challenge of Rule Eight [what you make of your life is up to you] is to create and own your own reality. The first moment you are able to do this is an awakening of sorts, since it means the demise of your unconscious life. I remember vividly the time in my life when this occurred ... Much to my surprise, rather than feeling relieved or

inspired, I felt depressed. After crying for what seemed like days, with hardly any idea why, I came to realize that the phase of my life in which I could float in the murky swamp of "I don't know" was coming to an end. Once I . . . knew what my purpose was, I had moved out of the safety zone of not knowing, otherwise known as "childhood" into the reality of the adult world. I knew that once I began consciously to own my life, it would be nearly impossible to sink back into oblivion. I wept tears of loss, for I had passed through a tunnel of maturity and left my unconscious life behind. Though sad, I was now ready to take command of my life.[21]

We all have the tools to create our own reality. A fundamental truth is that our external resources do not determine our success or failure. Rather, belief in ourselves and our willingness to act on those beliefs determine our destiny. What you make of your life, and whether you take your career to the Nth degree, is 100 percent up to you. I hope that this is as inspiring as it is scary. I know it was for me. Ultimately, I hope you choose inspiration over fear, action over inaction, and engagement over complacency. If you consciously choose to do what it takes, then I have no doubt that you can and will take your career and life from stuck to unstoppable.

ACKNOWLEDGMENTS

WRITING A BOOK, I have discovered, is not for the faint of heart. More times than I care to admit, I pushed back on deadlines, slept until noon when I could have been writing, and otherwise hoped the words would magically leap from my brain and onto the page. Without the constant support, guidance, and help from the people in my life who love me and see the best in me even when I can only see what's lacking, this book would never have been conceived of, let alone finished.

I have to, in the least cheesy-Oscar-acceptance-speech way, be first and foremost thankful to God for the vision and inspiration for my life. He gave me the strength to leave an environment where my purpose was going unfulfilled, create a system for others to do the same, and write a book about the process. If I didn't believe in a reason for being alive, all of this would be moot.

Mom . . . what can I say to encompass all that you are to me and my life and my work? Thank you for the "good morning" text messages that motivate me to get out of bed, for being my first "employee" when I couldn't afford to even feed myself, and for your tireless encouragement of me to put this important message out in the world. I can honestly say that I would be lost without you, and this book and my business are better off because you were involved. Thank you.

Dad, wherever you are zipping around the universe, I miss you. I'll never forget the day I was going to call you and Mom to say that I wanted to quit Wall Street. Mom was trying to hold the party line of "you can't quit a job without another job," but when you heard how miserable I was, you said, "Honey, run, don't walk, out of that office. We just want you to be happy." Those words resound in my mind any time I feel doubt or fear in my business and wonder if I would have been better off staying at the bank. You were right. And I will keep running until my legs give out from under me.

To two significant Matts—Matt M. and Matt E.—I owe you for the courage and motivation to leave my unfulfilling job and begin the search for my ideal career. Matt M., thanks for reminding me of the best version of myself that day on the steps outside of that wedding reception. Matt E., thank you for putting my two and a half years into perspective and encouraging me by being my best friend and champion.

To my closest friends from Connecticut, who had to listen to me complain constantly about work—Mary, Heather, Sarah, Courtney, and Kevin—I'm sorry. My relationships with you were the best part of my life back then, and I wouldn't have made it through that time without you.

To anyone I've worked with over the past five years, especially my earliest clients, thank you for putting your faith in me. The creation of the Nth Degree was evolutionary, and you helped me sculpt this proven process before I even knew what it would become. Thank you for the honor of allowing me into your life and sharing the journey with me. Please know that your stories, examples, and the ripple effects of living your best life will impact countless people after you.

My amazing team at Page Two! Trena, thank you for your patience and for seeing my ultimate vision before I could see it. To Kendra for helping me put my ideas into words and those words coherently onto a page. To everyone on the design team who seemed to intuitively know how to take my poorly worded concept and turn it into a beautiful reality. I can honestly say that without your motivation (and dead-lines!) this book would not exist. Ask anyone who knows me. I've been talking about writing a book for almost ten years.

To all of you out there pursuing your dreams: you're an inspiration that this world needs. Whether you're in the initial steps of discovering your true value, or you've moved on to defining your Olympic-gold-medal-level profession, or you're already driving your career destiny, you are single-handedly making the world around you a better place. As Marianne Williamson wrote in *A Return to Love*, "As we let our own light shine, we unconsciously give others permission to do the same." Keep shining. You will have an unknowable impact.

Most of all, thank *you* for taking the time to read this book.

NOTES

1   Russell Huber, "Become Who You Want to Be: Using Simple Tools Available to All Catholics" (PowerPoint presentation, Young Catholic Professionals, Dallas, Texas, January 13, 2015).

2   Ibid.

3   Rhonda Byrne, *The Secret* (New York: Atria Books; Hillsboro, OR: Beyond Words, 2018).

4   See, for example, Angela Chen, "Largest U.S. Twin Study Probes Whether Nature or Nurture Makes Us Sick," *The Verge*, January 16, 2019, theverge.com/2019/1/16/18185613/health-genetics-environment -nature-nurture-science; Jane E. Brody, "What Twins Can Teach Us about Nature vs. Nurture," *New York Times*, August 20, 2018, nytimes .com/2018/08/20/well/family/what-twins-can-teach-us-about-nature -vs-nurture.html.

5   Carol Dweck, *Mindset: The New Psychology of Success* (New York: Ballantine Books, 2016).

6   Chérie Carter-Scott, *If Life Is a Game, These Are the Rules: Ten Rules for Being Human as Introduced in Chicken Soup for the Soul* (New York: Harmony Books, 1998).

7   Michael Ellsberg, *The Education of Millionaires: Everything You Don't Learn in College about How to Be Successful* (New York: Penguin Group, 2012).

8   See, for example, Gina Bell, "At Least 70% of Jobs Aren't Even Listed—Here's How to Up Your Chances of Getting a Great New Gig," *Business Insider*, April 10, 2017, businessinsider.com/at-least-70-of -jobs-are-not-even-listed-heres-how-to-up-your-chances-of-getting -a-great-new-gig-2017-4; Wendy Kaufman, "A Successful Job Search: It's All about Networking," NPR, February 3, 2011, npr.org/2011/ 02/08/133474431/a-successful-job-search-its-all-about-networking;

Diana Rau, "80% of Jobs Are Not on Job Boards: Here's How to Find Them," *Forbes*, October 2, 2017, forbes.com/sites/dianatsai/2017/10/02/80-of-jobs-are-not-on-job-boards-heres-how-to-find-them/#1590334cd455.

9   Jeff Hoffman, "The Ultimate Guide to Prospecting: How Many Touchpoints, When, and What Type," HubSpot, accessed February 14, 2020, blog.hubspot.com/sales/the-ultimate-guide-to-prospecting-how-many-touchpoints-when-and-what-type.

10 Peter Sims, *Little Bets: How Breakthrough Ideas Emerge from Small Discoveries* (New York: Simon & Schuster, 2011).

11 Mark Manson, "7 Strange Questions That Help You Find Your Life Purpose," Mark Manson (website), accessed February 15, 2020, markmanson.net/life-purpose.

12 Nassim Nicholas Taleb, "Life Is about Execution rather than Purpose," Facebook post, March 15, 2013, facebook.com/nntaleb/posts/life-is-about-execution-rather-than-purpose/10151393579368375.

13 Og Mandino, *The Greatest Salesman in the World: You Can Change Your Life with the Priceless Wisdom of Ten Ancient Scrolls Handed Down for Thousands of Years* (New York: Bantam, 1983).

14 Stephen R. Covey, *First Things First* (New York: Free Press, 2003).

15 Marianne Williamson, *A Return to Love: Reflections on the Principles of A Course in Miracles* (New York: HarperPerennial, 1992).

16 Elizabeth Gilbert, *Big Magic: Creative Living beyond Fear* (New York: Riverhead Books, 2015).

17 Bronnie Ware, "Regrets of the Dying," Bronnie Ware (website), accessed February 15, 2020, bronnieware.com/blog/regrets-of-the-dying.

18 Tim Ferriss, "Why You Should Define Your Fears instead of Your Goals," TED2017, April 2017, 13:14, ted.com/talks/tim_ferriss_why_you_should_define_your_fears_instead_of_your_goals.

19 Agnes de Mille, *Martha: The Life and Work of Martha Graham* (New York: Random House, 1991).

20 Tracy Timm, "Being OPEN to Change," TEDxMarcusHighSchool, July 5, 2016, 16:31, tracytimm.com/qtvideo/ted-talk.

21 Chérie Carter-Scott, *If Life Is a Game, These Are the Rules.*

ABOUT THE AUTHOR

TRACY TIMM IS the founder of The Nth Degree® Career Academy, the proven career clarity system that helps high-potential professionals discover, define, and drive careers they love. She has a degree in behavioral psychology from Yale University and studied design thinking with the founder of the d.school at Stanford University. Tracy left a successful but unsatisfying career in finance, traveled once around the world on Semester at Sea, and discovered her ideal career. For more than five years, she has applied these lessons in her career advisory work with hundreds of individuals and over 100 fast-growing companies. Tracy lives in Dallas, Texas.

tracytimm.com
nthdegree.tracytimm.com